Maneuver Warfare Handbook

Westview Special Studies

The concept of Westview Special Studies is a response to the continuing crisis in academic and informational publishing. Library budgets are being diverted from the purchase of books and used for data banks, computers, micromedia, and other methods of information retrieval. Interlibrary loan structures further reduce the edition sizes required to satisfy the needs of the scholarly community. Economic pressures on university presses and the few private scholarly publishing companies have greatly limited the capacity of the industry to properly serve the academic and research communities. As a result, many manuscripts dealing with important subjects, often representing the highest level of scholarship, are no longer economically viable publishing projects--or, if accepted for publication, are typically subject to lead times ranging from one to three years.

Westview Special Studies are our practical solution to the problem. As always, the selection criteria include the importance of the subject, the work's contribution to scholarship, and its insight, originality of thought, and excellence of exposition. We accept manuscripts in camera-ready form, typed, set, or word processed according to specifications laid out in our comprehensive manual, which contains straightforward instructions and sample pages. The responsibility for editng and proofreading lies with the author or sponsoring institution, but our editorial staff is always available to answer questions and provide guidance.

The result is a book printed on acid-free paper and bound in sturdy, library-quality soft covers. We manufacture these books ourselves using equipment that does not require a lengthy make-ready process and that allows us to publish first editions of 300 to 1000 copies and to reprint even smaller quantities as needed. Thus, we can produce Special Studies quickly and can keep even very specialized books in print as long as there is a demand for them.

About the Book and Author

Maneuver warfare, often controversial and requiring operational and tactical innovation, poses perhaps the most important doctrinal questions currently facing the conventional military forces of the United States. The purpose of maneuver warfare is to defeat the enemy by disrupting his ability to react, rather than by physical destruction of forces. This book develops and explains the theory of maneuver warfare and offers specific tactical, operational, and organizational recommendations for improving ground combat forces. The author translates concepts--too often vaguely stated in discussions of maneuver warfare--into concrete doctrine. Although the book uses the Marine Corps as a model, the concepts, tactics, and doctrine discussed apply to any ground combat force.

William S. Lind is an advisor on military affairs to U.S. Senator Gary Hart, president of the Military Reform Institute, and a Resident Scholar at the Institute for Government and Politics of the Free Congress Foundation.

Maneuver Warfare Handbook

William S. Lind

Routledge
Taylor & Francis Group
New York London

Westview Special Studies in Military Affairs

First published 1985 by Westview Press

Published 2018 by Routledge
52 Vanderbilt Avenue, New York, NY 10017
2 Park Square, Milton Park, Abingdon, Oxon OX14 4RN

Routledge is an imprint of the Taylor & Francis Group, an informa business

Copyright © 1985 Taylor & Francis

Library of Congress Catalog Number: 84-20934

ISBN 13: 978-0-86531-862-5 (pbk)

Composition for this book was provided by the author

Contents

Acknowledgments

First and foremost, I owe a great debt to Captain R. S. Moore, USMC, who not only provided much of the material on which Chapters III and IV are based, but indeed first suggested that this book be written. Colonel John C. Studt, USMC (ret.) not only provided a very generous Foreword, he was also of great assistance in reviewing the draft, as were Colonel Michael D. Wyly, USMC, Colonel John Boyd, USAF (ret.), Major Kenneth Estes, USMC and Major William Woods, USMC. Colonel Wyly also provided an excellent appendix to the text in the form of his lectures on tactics delivered to the Amphibious Warfare School in 1981-82. Last but in no way least I owe a major debt to my typists, Mrs. Barbara Shortridge and Ms. Sandra Erb, who succeeded in turning my disorganized drafts and impossible handwriting into a presentable paper, and SSgt. Les Amen, USMC, who drew the maps.

For any errors in the book, as well as for any passages at which some may take offense (as some invariably will), I take full and sole responsibility.

William S. Lind

Foreword

Colonel John C. Studt, USMC (Ret.)

The author of this book has never served a day of active military duty, and he has never been shot at, although there are no doubt some senior officers who would like to remedy that latter deficiency. Yet he demonstrates an amazing understanding of the art of war, as have only a small handful of military thinkers I have come across in my career.

I served over 31 years active duty with the Marine Corps, saw combat in both Korea and Vietnam, and attended service schools from The Basic School to the National War College. Yet only toward the end of my military career did I realize how little I really understood the art of war. Even as a Pfc in Korea, after being med-evaced along with most of my platoon after a fruitless frontal assault against superior North Korean forces, it seemed to me there had to be a better way to wage war. Seventeen years later, commanding a battalion at Khe Sanh, I was resolved that none of my Marines would die for lack of superior combat power. But we were still relying on the concentration of superior firepower to win--essentially still practicing Grant's attrition warfare. And we were still doing frontal assaults!

When I first heard Bill Lind speak, I must confess I resented a mere civilian expressing criticism of the way our beloved Corps did things. After all, he was not one of us, he had not shed blood with us in battle, he was not a brother. And I had strong suspicions that he would have difficulty passing the PFT. But what he said made sense! For the first time I was personally hearing someone advocate an approach to war that was based on intellectual innovation rather than sheer material superiority: mission-type orders, surfaces and gaps, and Schwerpunkt, instead of the rigid formulas and checklists that we normally associate with our training and doctrine. It was a stimulating experience! Through Lind's articulation, years of my own reading of military history began to make a lot more sense.

But why all this from a civilian instead of a professional soldier? In fact, the entire movement for military reform is driven largely by civilian intellectuals, not military officers--one notable exception being retired Air Force Colonel

John Boyd. When you think about it, this is not surprising. We have never institutionalized a system that encourages innovative ideas or criticism from subordinates. Proposing significant change is frequently viewed as criticism of superiors, since they are responsible for the way things are, and borders on disloyalty if not insubordination. So it is not surprising that the movement for reform comes from outside the military establishment.

And it is not surprising that the author of this book should be in the forefront of the reform movement and president of the Military Reform Institute. A magna cum laude history major from Dartmouth, Bill Lind was gifted with a brilliant mind and a rare talent for translating the lessons of history into practical application. He has studied and researched war, and has delved into the minds of the more successful practitioners, as no professional military officer I know of has done. His crusade to sell "maneuver warfare" has made him well known--if not well loved--by those who read the Marine Corps Gazette and other current military literature.

In this handbook Bill Lind lays out the concept of maneuver warfare in clear, understandable language, and he supports and illustrates his theories with excellent historical examples. What he has produced is a text book on how to conduct warfare, and it calls for a totally different approach than we teach in our schools today. Yet it is no more than a compilation of theories proven on a hundred battlefields throughout history. But it would seem that only the Germans and Israelis have institutionalized the practice of maneuver warfare in recent times.

B. H. Liddell Hart once remarked that "The only thing harder than getting a new idea into the military mind is to get an old one out." In 1925, when he was expounding such heretical theories as the "indirect approach," the American General Service Schools' "Review of Current Military Literature" dismissed one of Liddell Hart's major works as: "Of negative value to the instructors at these schools." I expect Marine Corps schools to receive this publication with similar enthusiasm. But I cannot believe a professional military officer would not benefit by reading it. For the first time in our history we face a potential enemy with superiority in men and material. Against such an enemy we cannot win with the firepower/attrition doctrine we embrace today. In this book Bill Lind offers an alternative.

Introduction

Although this book has been written to be helpful to anyone interested in land warfare, it is addressed primarily to Marines. Most Marines have already heard or read something about maneuver warfare. It has been the subject of many articles in the <u>Marine Corps Gazette</u>. The 2nd Marine Division, under Major General A. M. Gray, Jr., adopted maneuver warfare as doctrine. General Gray established a Maneuver Warfare Board to help spread the concept throughout the division, and also carried out a series of maneuver warfare field exercises at Ft. Pickett, Virginia. The Junior Officers' Tactical Symposium in the 1st Marine Division has also worked to understand and develop maneuver warfare ideas. For a brief period, maneuver tactics were taught as doctrine at Amphibious Warfare School.

Nor is maneuver warfare just of academic interest to Marines. 2nd Battalion 8th Marines, under Lt. Col. Ray Smith, used it on Grenada. As this author wrote in a Military Reform Institute report:

> Although the Marine units on Grenada never met much opposition, they did face a number of confusing and urgent situations, which they seem to have handled well. Reflecting their parent 2nd Marine Division's emphasis on maneuver warfare, they did not attempt to follow a rigid plan but rather adapted swiftly to circumstances as they changed. The speed with which the Marines acted and moved was decisive in one interesting case. The Grenadians had about one platoon of troops defending St. George's, which ultimately did not fight. Part of the reason it did not was explained by a senior Grenadian officer after his capture. He said the Marines appeared so swiftly where they were not expected that the Grenadian Army's high command in the capital was convinced resistance was hopeless, the best possible outcome in maneuver warfare.[1]

Despite all the attention, maneuver warfare remains a subject of much confusion. Some say, "It's just a fancy new name for what we've always done." Others call it "common sense tactics," as if all it requires is a bit of common sense. Terms such as mission-type orders, reconnaissance pull, surfaces and gaps, and Schwerpunkt are thrown around with little understanding of their meaning or significance.

The purpose of this handbook is to try to clear up the confusion. It has been written as a ready reference for field Marines, not an academic monograph. It seeks to define and explain the basic concepts and terminology of maneuver warfare; to show some practical ways to apply maneuver theory; and to spur further thinking, reading, and writing on the subject by Marines.

Why should Marines care about maneuver warfare? Why should anyone bother to write a book on the subject especially for Marines? Maneuver warfare has special meaning and potential for the Marine Corps, for three reasons:

First, the Marine Corps has traditionally been an innovator. In the 1920s and 1930s, when the common wisdom said amphibious warfare was impossible under modern conditions, Marines responded with some uncommon wisdom. They studied history with great care, thought about what they had read, and gave their imaginations free rein. They developed new amphibious concepts, doctrine and techniques. With strong support from their Commandants, they took their new ideas to the field and tested them.

When war came in 1941, the new ideas were ready, and they worked. As General Alexander A. Vandegrift said, "Despite its outstanding record as a combat force in the past war, the Marine Corps' far greater contribution to victory was doctrinal: that is, the fact that the basic amphibious doctrine which carried Allied troops over every beachhead of World War II had been largely shaped -- often in the face of uninterested or doubting military orthodoxy -- by U.S. Marines, and mainly between 1922 and 1935."[2]

Second, Marines know they are likely to fight outnumbered. In Europe, the Warsaw Pact fields more combat units than NATO. In the Persian Gulf, nations such as Iran and Iraq have armies of 500,000 or more men. In other parts of the Middle East, in Asia, and even in Latin America our shortage of amphibious lift, the relatively small size of the Corps and the many commitments facing the Army mean that Marines could be sent into battle against a numerically superior enemy.

History suggests God is on the side of the bigger battalions -- unless the smaller battalions have a better idea. A slugging match against someone much stronger than yourself is never very promising. Even if you win, the cost is usually high. But if you can use judo against your larger opponent, if you can psych him out, throw him off balance, and use his own momentum against him, you can win, and often you can win quickly and at small cost.

Maneuver warfare can be thought of as military judo. It is a way of fighting smart, of out-thinking an opponent you may not be able to overpower with brute strength. As such, it offers Marines the best hope of winning the battles, campaigns and wars they may face in the future.

Third, to a Marine, nothing is more important than combat. In some other services, the most important things sometimes seem to be engineering or management or high technology. Marines have not fallen into these traps. They do not introduce themselves at

cocktail parties as "middle managers." They see themselves as
fighters, as warriors, and they want to be the best of the breed.
They are willing to work, study and, if necessary, "bet their
bars" in order to be the best.

That is what this book is about -- combat, and how to win in
combat. That is what maneuver warfare is about. And that is why
this book has been written for Marines.

1
The Theory of Maneuver Warfare

Maneuver warfare is not new. It probably dates from the first time a caveman surprised an enemy from behind instead of meeting him club-to-club. The first clear case in recorded history was the battle of Leuctra in 371 B.C. The Thebans won that battle, thanks to a surprise strike against the right flank of the rigid Spartan phalanx. Hannibal's defeat of the Romans at Cannae in 216 B.C., one of the most decisive tactical victories of all time, was an example of maneuver warfare. Modern history offers many examples: Rosecranz at Chattanooga, Grant at Vicksburg, and Jackson's Valley Campaign in the American Civil War; German infiltration tactics in the offensive of 1918; the World War II Blitzkrieg; and General Sharon's attack across the Suez Canal in 1973.

Why are all these cases of "maneuver warfare"? What is "maneuver"? Sometimes the word maneuver is used as a synonym for movement, such as in references to "fire and maneuver" in small-unit tactics. A traditional definition is offered by Soviet Colonel F. D. Sverdlov in a recent study, <u>Tactical Maneuver</u>. "Maneuver...is organized movement of troops (forces) during combat operations to a new axis (line) and region for the purpose of taking an advantageous position relative to the enemy in order to deliver a decisive strike."[1]

But when used in the phrase "maneuver warfare," maneuver means much more. It is what all these cases--Leuctra, Cannae, Vicksburg, the German 1918 offensive, the Suez Canal crossing and many, many others--have in common. The theory of maneuver warfare must answer the question: What was the essence of success in all of these cases?

Only recently has someone suggested a convincing answer. The man is a retired Air Force colonel and fighter pilot named John Boyd. Colonel Boyd's development of the theory of maneuver warfare began, not with ground battles, but with a study of some mock air-to-air combat exercises (conducted at Nellis Air Force Base in 1974) that led him back to the study of air-to-air combat during the Korean war. American aviators were very successful in that conflict. They achieved a 10:1 kill ratio over their North Korean and Chinese opponents. Colonel Boyd began his study with the question: "How and why did we do so well?"

4

He noted that in several traditional measures of aircraft performance, the principal Communist fighter, the MiG-15, was superior to the American F-86. It could climb and accelerate faster, and it had a better sustained turn rate. But in two less obvious measures of aircraft performance, the F-86 was much superior to the MiG. First, the pilot could see out much better. The F-86's bubble canopy gave its pilot very good outward vision, while the MiG's faired canopy made it difficult to see out. Second, the F-86 had high-powered and highly effective hydraulic controls and the MiG did not. This meant that while the MiG could do many individual actions--including turn, climb, and accelerate--better than the F-86, the F-86 could transition from one action to another much more quickly than the MiG.

Using these two superiorities, the American pilots developed a tactical approach that forced the MiG into a series of actions. Each time the action changed, the F-86 gained a time advantage, because the F-86 pilot could see more quickly how the situation had changed and he could also make his aircraft shift more quickly to a new action. With each change, the MiG's actions became more inappropriate, until they were so inappropriate that the MiG gave the F-86 a good firing opportunity. Often, it appeared the MiG pilot realized what was happening to him and panicked, which made the American pilot's job all the easier.

Later Colonel Boyd began studying ground combat to see if there were situations similar to that he had found in the air war over Korea. He found that in battles, campaigns and wars like Leuctra, Vicksburg and France in 1940, a similar thing seemed to have happened. One side had presented the other with a sudden, unexpected change or a series of such changes to which it could not adjust in a timely manner. As a result, it was defeated, and it was generally defeated at small cost to the victor. Often, the losing side had been physically stronger than the winner. And often, the same sort of panic and paralysis the North Korean and Chinese pilots had shown seemed to occur.

Colonel Boyd asked himself, what did all these cases have in common? His answer was what is now called the Boyd Theory, which is the theory of maneuver warfare. The briefing Colonel Boyd gives to explain his theory, "Patterns of Conflict," takes over five hours. But, at the cost of missing some of the subtleties and the supporting historical evidence in the briefing, it can be summarized as follows.

Conflict can be seen as time-competitive observation-orientation-decision-action cycles. Each party to a conflict begins by observing. He observes himself, his physical surroundings and his enemy. On the basis of his observation, he orients, that is to say, he makes a mental image or "snapshot" of his situation. On the basis of this orientation, he makes a decision. He puts the decision into effect, i.e., he acts. Then, because he assumes his action has changed the situation, he observes again, and starts the process anew. His actions follow this cycle, sometimes called the "Boyd Cycle" or "OODA Loop."

If one side in a conflict can consistently go through the Boyd Cycle faster than the other, it gains a tremendous advantage. By the time the slower side acts, the faster side is doing something different from what he observed, and his action is inappropriate. With each cycle, the slower party's action is inappropriate by a larger time margin. Even though he desperately strives to do something that will work, each action is less useful than its predecessor; he falls farther and farther behind. Ultimately, he ceases to be effective.

This is what happened to the Spartans at Leuctra, the Romans at Cannae, the French in 1940 and the Communist fighter pilots over Korea. Sometimes, a single action was enough, as in the Thebans' oblique attack at Leuctra. Sometimes, as in the Blitzkrieg or air combat over Korea, a series of OODA Loops was required. But whether it was through a single action or a large number, the essence of what happened was the same.

The Boyd Theory defines what is meant by the word "maneuver" in the term "maneuver warfare." Maneuver means Boyd Cycling the enemy, being consistently faster through however many OODA Loops it takes until the enemy loses his cohesion-- until he can no longer fight as an effective, organized force.

Sometimes, a Boyd Cycled enemy panics or becomes passive. This is an ideal outcome for the victor, because a panicked or passive enemy can be annihilated or captured at the lowest cost in friendly casualties. At other times, the outmaneuvered enemy may continue to fight as individuals or small units. But because he can no longer act effectively as a force, he is comparatively easy to destroy. A good example of a panicked enemy can be seen in Rommel's success at the battle of Caporetto in World War I, where with a force of about a battalion he took more than 10,000 Italian prisoners. At Cannae, the Romans continued to fight as individuals. But in both situations, the basis of victory was the same: one side Boyd Cycled the other.

If the object in maneuver warfare is to move through OODA Loops faster than the enemy, what do you need to do? How can you be consistently faster? Much of the rest of this book is an effort to address that question. But in terms of general theory, the following points are worth thinking about:

1. Only a decentralized military can have a fast OODA Loop. If the observations must be passed up a chain of command, the orientation made and the decision taken at a high level, and the command for action then transmitted back down the chain, the OODA Loop is going to be slow. As the Israeli military historian Martin Van Creveld has observed:

> From Plato to NATO, the history of command in war consists of an endless quest for certainty. Certainty concerning the state and intentions of the enemy's forces; certainty concerning the manifold factors which together constitute the environment, from the weather and the terrain to radioactivity and the presence of chemical warfare agents; and, last but definitely not least, certainty concerning the state and activities of one's own forces... historical commanders have always faced the choice between two basic ways of coping with uncertainty. One was to construct an army of automatons following the orders of a single man, allowed to do only that which could be controlled; the other, to design organizations

and operations in such a way as to enable the former to carry out the latter without the need for continuous control. ...the second of these methods has, by and large, proved more successful than the first; and...the ongoing revolution in the technology of command notwithstanding, this is likely to remain so in the future and indeed so long as war itself exists.[2]

2. Maneuver warfare means you will not only accept confusion and disorder and operate successfully within it, through decentralization, you will also generate confusion and disorder. The "reconnaissance pull" (see Chapters II and III) tactics of the German Blitzkrieg were inherently disorderly. Higher headquarters could neither direct nor predict the exact path of the advance. But the multitude of German reconnaissance thrusts generated massive confusion among the French in 1940. Each was reported as a new attack. The Germans seemed to be everywhere, and the French, whose system demanded certainty before making any decisions, were paralyzed.

3. All patterns, recipes and formulas are to be avoided. The enemy must not be able to predict your actions. If your tactics follow predictable patterns, the enemy can easily cut inside your OODA Loop. If he can predict what you will do, he will be waiting for you.

This is why it is so hard to tell someone how to do maneuver warfare. There is no formula you can learn. When someone says, "Cut all the bull about theory; just tell me what to do," you can't. You can talk about how to think, and about some useful techniques. But you can't give new formulas to replace the ones currently taught at Marine Corps schools.

Instead of a checklist or a cookbook, maneuver warfare requires commanders who can sense more than they can see, who understand the opponent's strengths and weaknesses and their own, and who can find the enemy's critical weaknesses in a specific situation (which is seldom easy). They must be able to create multiple threats and keep the enemy uncertain as to which is real. They must be able to see their options in the situation before them, constantly create new options, and shift rapidly among options as the situation develops. General Hermann Balck, one of the most successful practitioners of maneuver warfare, said:

> I'm against the school approach that says, "In accordance with the ideas of the General Staff, in this situation you must do thus and such." On the contrary, you must proceed as dictated by the personalities involved and the particulars of the situation. For instance, you are attacking at 7 o'clock in the morning and you have given clear tasks to each of your divisions: this one takes this objective, the next one grabs this, the third does nothing except to protect the left flank. At the next attack opportunity you may have an almost identical situation, but everything must be changed completely because your most competent division commander has been killed in the meanwhile.

Therefore, one of the first principles has to be: There can be no fixed schemes. Every scheme, every pattern is wrong. No two situations are identical. That is why the study of military history can be extremely dangerous.

Another principle that follows from this is: Never do the same thing twice. Even if something works well for you once, by the second time the enemy will have adapted. So you have to think up something new.

No one thinks of becoming a great painter simply by imitating Michaelangelo. Similarly, you can't become a great military leader just by imitating so and so. It has to come from within. In the last analysis, military command is an art: one man can do it and most will never learn. After all, the world is not full of Raphaels either.[3]

2
Tactics and Operations

If maneuver warfare cannot be done by formulas and recipes, how can it be done? To help answer this question, you might want to look at some pictures of maneuver warfare.

Picture #1: The expanding torrent. B. H. Liddell Hart, the famous British military historian and theorist, drew an analogy between a maneuver warfare attack and flowing water. He wrote:

> If we watch a torrent bearing down on each successive bank or earthen dam in its path, we see that it first beats against the obstacle, feeling and testing it at all points.
> Eventually, it finds a small crack at some point. Through this crack pour the first driblets of water and rush straight on.
> The pent-up water on each side is drawn towards the breach. It swirls through and around the flanks of the breach, wearing away the earth on each side and so widening the gap.
> Simultaneously the water behind pours straight through the breach between the side eddies which are wearing away the flanks. Directly it has passed through it expands to widen once more the onrush of the torrent. Thus as the water pours through in ever-increasing volume the onrush of the torrent swells to its original proportions, leaving in turn each crumbling obstacle behind it.
> Thus Nature's forces carry out the ideal attack, automatically maintaining the speed, the breadth, and the continuity of the attack.[1]

Picture #2: German defensive tactics in 1917. During the winter of 1916-17, the Germans abandoned what we think of as the classic First World War defense, where men were closely packed into trenches and fought to hold every inch of ground. Instead, they adopted an elastic defense in depth, a defense that reflected maneuver warfare. Captain Timothy Lupfer discusses it in his excellent study, The Dynamics of Doctrine:

> The trenches were necessary for daily living, but once detected they were lathered with preparatory fire and barrages. Deep dugouts in forward areas were also

9

impractical, for soldiers remained in them too long after the enemy barrage lifted and were often captured. Therefore, under heavy fire, the forward German soldiers evacuated their trenches and shifted from shell hole to shell hole, avoiding concentrations of fire and escaping the detection of aerial artillery spotters.

The Allied advance would first encounter resistance from pockets of German survivors in shell holes. Having been concealed from aerial observation, units positioned on the reverse slope would then open fire unexpectedly. The Allies would also encounter fortified strongpoints... built to provide for all-around defense and they engaged the attackers, whenever possible, with devastating enfilade fire. The strongpoints would remain fighting even if cut off by the enemy advance.

The ideal scenario was:

A fragmented, exhausted Allied attack force reaches the battle zone. They hope that their thorough artillery preparation has killed all the Germans, but they encounter several Germans firing at them from shell holes in the torn ground. Sudden fire from the German main line of resistance has slowed the Allies and their scheduled artillery barrage has crept forward without them, according to a timed sequence of fire they cannot modify. They feel helpless without artillery support. The Allies finally have taken the main line of resistance at great cost, but now they are in unfamiliar ground, under fire from concealed enemy machine gunners and riflemen. German artillery, which the Allies expected to destroy in the preparatory fires, now appears very active. The Germans concentrate their artillery fire behind the Allied advanced units, cutting them off from reinforcements and supplies. For the next few minutes, the Allies have a tenuous hold on a few acres of ground, but by advancing into the battle zone, the Allies are most vulnerable, and have exposed themselves to the counterattack, the soul of the German defense. The immediate counterattack, well coordinated with accurate artillery fire, destroys, captures or ejects the Allied unit before it can consolidate its gains. The coherence of the German defense is restored...

In its most developed form, the defense had designated counterattack forces throughout the zones. In the outpost zone, local commanders designated counterattack squads. In the battle zone, commanders designated counterattack companies. . . The regiment's reserve battalion was part of the division reserve, in which each remaining battalion from each frontline regiment served as a counterattack battalion, striking from the rear of the battle zone. Behind these counterattack battalions were the reserves of the field army (entire counterattack divisions), and OHL itself (Supreme Army Headquarters) retained control of additional counterattack divisions.

The defense thus assumed a very aggressive and potentially offensive character. The best time for counterattack was the period of confusion when the attacker had not yet consolidated his position or reorganized his forces. Timing was critical.[2]

Picture #3: German assault tactics on the Eastern Front, 1942. Following an abortive armored attack on a Soviet defensive position, an infantry task force cleared the strongpoint using assault teams and follow-on reinforcements.

The left wing was formed by the seasoned 6th Armored Reconnaissance Battalion, the right by the 1st Armored Infantry Battalion of the 114th Infantry Regiment (Mechanized). The two battalions were reinforced by engineer assault detachments, flame-thrower teams, and mine-clearing details. The tanks and remaining armored infantry elements were assembled in the rear between Zalivsky and Klykov, where they stayed in reserve, ready to follow up the assault force. At 0800 on 17 December the massed guns of the artillery regiment opened fire. As the hail of shells came down on the ridge it obliterated the Russian observation post. The dried-out steppe grass burned fiercely and reddish clouds of dust enveloped the whole ridge, depriving the Russians of all visibility. After a short time, however, the fires died out because a light snowfall prevented them from spreading.

Meanwhile, the first German assault wave moved up to the ridge. When a signal flare was set off to indicate it was entering the Russian defensive positions, the artillery fire was shifted. The assault detachments had opened a gap at the center of the ridge. The difficult task of ferreting out the enemy force dug in on the ridge had thus begun.

Several squadrons of German dive bombers, flying in relays, came over and headed in the direction of Verkhniy Kumskiy, where they blasted Russian artillery positions, silencing one battery after another. Directly overhead, Messerschmitts and Ratas tangled in dogfights, during which three of the Russian fighters were shot down near the ridge.

Paying little heed to the air action, the assault forces fanned out from the initial point of penetration and moved forward. Machine gunners and sharpshooting riflemen stalked the hidden Russians like game and fired well-aimed bullets at anything that moved. Whenever Russians from a nearby foxhole returned the fire, they were silenced by a well-placed hand grenade. The fortified positions were neutralized by the flame-thrower teams. Whenever a particularly fanatic Russian force could not be flushed out by the assault troops they fired a signal flare to pinpoint the target for the German artillery pieces and mortars.

By noon the reconnaissance battalion had cleared all enemy forces from its zone of action, and an hour later the armored infantry battalion had done likewise on the eastern part of the ridge. An attack on Verkhniy Kumskiy could be envisaged.[3]

Today, Marines learn tactics as a series of formulas, starting at The Basic School. Tactics are defined as the "how to" of things like a penetration, an attack, coordination of supporting arms and so on. Ability is measured in checklist-type tests like the CAX and the MCCRES. In 1983, the final exam in tactics at Amphibious Warfare School was all true/false or multiple choice, and included such questions as "The ___ stove is the primary heat source for the Ten Man Tent," and "The ___ is the basic ski technique utilized in a controlled movement downhill."

Maneuver warfare is not very concerned with names of stoves and skiing techniques. It looks at tactics differently. A useful definition of tactics in maneuver warfare is:

Tactics is a process of combining two elements, techniques and education, through three mental "filters" or reference points -- mission-type orders, the focus of effort or Schwerpunkt, and the search for enemy surfaces and gaps--with the object of producing a unique approach for the specific enemy, time and place.

What does a careful look at this definition show? First, it says tactics is not a thing, but a process -- especially a mental process. It is a way of doing something. It is not just a certain type of attack or defense, it is also why you chose that particular attack or defense. Tactics is not just your decision as a commander, it is how you come to your decision--your method.

Second, the definition says the goal of the process is a unique approach. You always want to do something different, something the enemy does not expect.

Third, you must consider the specific enemy, time and place. Everything must be according to the situation. Each situation is different. One enemy behaves differently from another -- Czechs or North Koreans or Syrians fight differently from Soviets. One Soviet division or regiment or company will fight differently from another. And the same enemy unit will fight differently on Thursday from the way it fought on Tuesday. What you do as a commander must take all these changes into account. What works one day will not work the next.

Fourth, tactics combines two basic elements, techniques and education. Techniques are things you can do by formula. They include how to aim a rifle, set up a machine gun, give an order, establish communications, call in fire support, gun crew drills, unit battle drills and so on. Excellence in techniques is very important in maneuver warfare! Some people have suggested maneuver warfare advocates do not care about techniques. This is flat wrong! A major difference between a military that can do maneuver warfare in combat and one that can only talk about it is excellence in techniques. Sloppy techniques slow down your Boyd Cycle and make your action ineffective.

But good techniques are not enough. The process that is tactics includes the art of selecting from among your techniques those which create that unique approach for the enemy, time and place. Education is the basis for doing that -- education not in what to do, but in how to think. Military history, war gaming, terrain walks and all other educational tools must be used by every officer to build his own military education. It is only the combination of techniques and education that enables an officer to do maneuver tactics. Education without excellence in techniques means action will not be timely or effective. But techniques without education means tactics will be formulistic, rigid, and predictable to the enemy.

What about the three "filters"? Perhaps the first question is, what is a "filter"? A filter is a mental reference point, a way to help shape and guide your thought process. We all have them. Some are conscious, some not. Three are very helpful in maneuver warfare tactics: mission-type orders, Schwerpunkt, and surfaces and gaps.

1. Mission-type orders. Mission-type orders are key to the decentralization necessary for a rapid Boyd Cycle. A mission-type order tells the subordinate commander what his superior wants to have accomplished. That is the mission. It leaves how to accomplish it largely up to the subordinate. As the subordinate's situation changes, he does what he thinks is necessary to bring about the result his superior wants. He informs his superior what he has done, but he does not wait for permission before he acts. What would happen to his Boyd Cycle if he did?

A useful way to think of mission-type orders is in terms of contracts between superior and subordinate.[4] There are two contracts. One is long-term. It is based on what we call the commander's intent. This is the commander's long-term vision of what he wants to have happen to the enemy, of the final result he wants. The subordinate needs to understand this two levels up. If he is a platoon commander, he needs to know the battalion commander's intent. If he is a company commander, he needs to know the brigade commander's intent, and so on. The "contract" is simple: the subordinate contracts to make his actions serve his superior's intent -- what is to be accomplished -- and the superior contracts to allow the subordinate great freedom of action in terms of how his intent is realized.

The mission is a shorter-term contract. It is a "slice" of the commander's intent, a slice small enough to be appropriate to the immediate situation of the subordinate unit. The contract is the same: the subordinate agrees to make his actions support the mission in return for wide-ranging freedom in selecting the means.

How far does this freedom of action go? The answer, as is so often the case in maneuver warfare, is that it depends on the situation. In some cases, the freedom of action granted the subordinate may be total. The superior may not specify anything more than the result to be achieved. For example, at one point during the fighting on the Golan Heights during the 1973 Mideast war, an Israeli commander received orders to block a Syrian armored brigade. That was the whole order -- don't let them through.[5]

At other times, the orders may be quite specific and detailed as far as the subordinate's initial actions are concerned. A good example is a deliberate attack on a prepared position. Jumping-off points, timing, and initial objectives will often be specified, and the subordinate will rightly be expected to do what he is told. But once the attack is underway and the situation begins changing rapidly, the subordinate will again be expected to adjust his actions to the changes on his own initiative, with appropriate reference to his superior's intent.

Under such a system, how do you avoid mistakes? You don't entirely. Mission-type orders and a "zero-defects mentality" are contradictory. Several years ago, a member of Congress told a German Army colonel that he wanted to organize his Congressional office on the basis of mission-type orders. The colonel replied, "That is very good, but I hope you realize it means allowing your staff to make mistakes." A maneuver warfare military believes it is better to have high levels of initiative among subordinate officers, with a resultant rapid Boyd Cycle, even if the price is some mistakes.

Doesn't the superior lose control if his subordinates have a great deal of freedom to make their own decisions? The historical record quickly shows this is not the case. Generals George Patton and Bruce Clark both used mission-type orders in World War II. The German army has used mission-type orders for over a century, yet it has not been an army that was "out of control." What changes is the way control is achieved. Instead of controlling by telling the subordinate what to do and then demanding constant reports to show he is doing it, control comes through the intent and the mission. Indeed, control is really replaced with guidance, while the intent and the mission "glue" the force together.

There are a number of misconceptions about mission-type orders. Some of the more common are:

"In a mission-type order, the battalion commander just orders his company commander to 'attack and seize hill 207.' He does not tell him how to do it." Sometimes, a mission-type order may tell you to take a specific piece of ground. But more often, it will tell you what your commander wants you to do to the enemy. Instead of "attack and seize hill 207," it will say, "attack the enemy in the left flank through hill 207." In this case, if the company commander sees that hill 207 is not the best route to the enemy's flank, he will take another route on his own authority. If possible, he will inform his battalion commander of the change in plans. But he will act first, inform later.

"A mission-type order just tells you to defeat the enemy." There is more to it than that in most cases. Your commander has a responsibility to think through a way to defeat the enemy, and to communicate that clearly to you. He must tell you, "here is what I want to do to the enemy." You must know what he has in mind, and think through what that means for your unit. Then you must make sure your subordinates understand what you are thinking.

"Mission-type orders mean you can do whatever you want." In many cases, you can largely "do what you want" in terms of means, but not ends. Your actions must always fit in with what your commander is trying to accomplish --with his intent and the mission. If he also suggests some means, you cannot disregard his suggestions, but if you find that the situation changes or is different from what your commander envisaged, you put the ends above the means and do what you think is appropriate.

What do mission orders look like? A historical example can help answer this.

In July of 1941 the 78th Infantry Division of the German Army had crossed the Dnieper about ten kilometers south of Mogilev, with orders to advance on the town of Krichev. The division commander, General Curt Gallenkamp, issued this order preparatory to an attack on July 25:

(1) Enemy forces numbering at least one Soviet division in the area south of Mogilev endanger the ordered advance of the division in the left flank. The enemy situation to the northeast, where heavily motorized traffic has been reported, is not yet clear.

(2) On the morning of 25 July, the 78th Division will attack and destroy the enemy group south of Mogilev. For the duration of the attack the division will be attached to VII Corps.

(3) For this purpose the following units will be assembled prior to 0600 hours on 25 July:

(a) The 195th Infantry with 4th Battery, 178th Artillery...It will be the mission of 195th Infantry to concentrate its main effort on pinning down the enemy on its front on both sides of the road to Mogilev and to push him steadily northward.

(b) The 238th Infantry...The task of the 238th Infantry will be to concentrate its main effort on the right, attack the enemy on its front and to drive him back. The regiment will direct its main attention to the prevention of any enemy action against the left flank of the 215th Infantry attacking on the right of the 238th Infantry.

(c) To the right of the boundary line separating it from the 238th Regiment, the 215th Regiment will organize its forces on both sides of the road leading northward to the Dnieper bend and echeloned to the right rear.

It will be the regiment's mission, by means of a powerful thrust northward as far as the Dnieper bend, to prevent Soviet forces stationed westward in the Dnieper bend from escaping eastward. The 238th Infantry will be responsible for protection of the left flank of the 215th Infantry. The speed of the 215th Regiment's advance will decide the success of the over-all attack.

(4) The commander of 178th Artillery will concentrate his entire fire power (less the 4th Battery, which is to be attached to 195th Infantry) to the rear of the right flank of the division in such a manner that the massed fire of the regiment can be observed while it first supports the attack of the 215th Infantry, and then the right flank of the 238th Regiment...

(5) By 0600, 25 July, the main body of the 178th Panzer Jaeger (anti-tank) Battalion will assembly in area (y) behind the 215th Infantry and to the right, in such a manner that it can repulse any armored assault against the attacking 215th Infantry Regiment. For this purpose it will reconnoiter in a northeasterly direction the enemy motorized forces which have been reported.

(6) The 178th Reconnaissance Battalion will reconnoiter in a general easterly direction in the area adjacent to the Panzer

Jaeger battalion and will protect the right flank of the attacking 78th Infantry Division...

(7) <u>Division Reserves</u>:

(a) The 238th Infantry Regiment must not commit the battalion held in reserve behind the right flank without my permission...

(8) The closing in assembly positions will be reported to me at my command post by 0600, 25 July.

(9) The beginning of the attack will be ordered on the morning of 25 July.

(10) During the division's attack I shall first be with the 238th Infantry Regiment, and later in the sector of 215th Infantry Regiment. The Division command radio station will accompany me wherever I go.

/s/ Gallenkamp
Generalleutnant
and Division Commander

On July 29, with the action well underway, new orders were required. With full confidence in the officers and troops under him, the division commander decided on a "double enveloping attack against enemy groups attacking from the north." For this purpose he issued the following individual orders:

(1) <u>By telephone to 195th Infantry Regiment</u>

The reinforced 195th Infantry (less its 3d Battalion), with 178th Engineer Battalion, 178th Panzer Jaeger Battalion, and the heavy weapons company of 178th Reconnaissance Battalion attached will attack from its left flank in the direction of Hill 95 north of Blagovichi and from there push foward toward the village of "Y".

All available motor vehicles will be used to form a mobile combat group which will skirt the enemy left flank and compress it by a thrust deep in its flank.

The 236th Infantry will envelop the right enemy flank. The combat group in Blagovichi will hold its present position and will be supported by 215th Infantry attacking from the west.

(2) <u>Radio message to 215th Infantry Regiment</u>

The division will destroy enemy through double envelopment. It will pin down and slowly force back the enemy on its front toward village Y. By making contact with the combat group in Blagovichi, which is being attacked by superior enemy forces, it will relieve this unit.

<u>Radio message to 238th Infantry Regiment</u>

The 238th Regimental Combat Group (minus first Battalion, 238th Infantry) will force a decision by enveloping the enemy's western flank from our left. Direction of attack of its own right flank is "Y" village.

The 1st Battalion, 238th Infantry, will fight its way through in the direction of Blagovichi and at 1400 will be at my disposal in the forest south of Blagovichi.

(3) <u>Oral Order to Commander, 178th Artillery Regiment</u>

Combat Group Blagovichi, under the commander of 178th Artillery, will hold its positions. Its most urgent mission is to relieve 178th Signal Battalion. Combat Group Chaussy, and the 215th and 238th Regimental Combat Groups will carry out an envelopment. The division headquarters will move its command post to a sunken road due east of the village near the road to Chaussy.

These orders show how the commander makes his intent known to his subordinates and gives them missions. They also show the wide latitude allowed to subordinates. How they accomplished their missions -- conducting an attack, relieving a unit that was under enemy pressure, enveloping one of the enemy's flanks, etc. -- was up to them.

The commentary on these orders makes some useful points:

> The manner in which the division commander gave his orders to his regimental commanders at Mogilev, namely by assigning missions, may in some cases cause surprise. The division commander used this manner of issuing orders during the entire 1941 campaign in Russia, because since the autumn of 1939 he and his division had become so close to each other, and because in his subordinate commanders he had men whose capabilities were best suited to this manner of issuing orders. The numerous great successes scored by the division prove that this was an effective method. In this respect, too, the ... examples prove that no rigid pattern should ever be followed in combat. Individual adaptation to given circumstances and a profound understanding of the psychology of subordinate commanders and troops are qualifications which are necessary to senior commanders. Frequently such characteristics are the key to success.[6]

The change to mission-type orders is a big one. Some Marine commanders will find it difficult to give their subordinates so much freedom of action. Senior commanders will have to make it clear that the days of "zero defects" are over. But most commanders will find the new freedom a breath of fresh air. And the mutual trust the "contracts" involve will be a welcome change from the constant checking and reporting that now take so much of a Marine officer's time.

2. The second "filter," and the third "glue" that holds activities together is the focus of effort or, to use the German term, <u>Schwerpunkt</u>. This is sometimes translated as "point of main effort," but such a translation is dangerous. It is not a point on a map. It is where the commander believes he can achieve a decision, and it translates into a unit, as in "<u>Schwerpunkt</u> is 2nd battalion."

When a unit is designated the focus of effort, all other units work to support it. It gets the artillery, air, and so on. The reserve is positioned to be able to exploit its success. Its neighbors each ask themselves, "What can I do to support the Schwerpunkt?"

The concept of Schwerpunkt is very important for any force that will fight outnumbered, because it enables it to direct all its power to one purpose. If it focuses all its effort to strike hard at one of the enemy's weak points, it can overthrow an opponent who is, in total strength, more powerful.

Schwerpunkt is not just the main attack (though the main attack is often at the Schwerpunkt). It is a conceptual focus, not just a physical one. All commanders refer to the Schwerpunkt, along with their superior's intent and the mission, in making their own decisions. Each makes sure his actions support the Schwerpunkt. This is why it is the third "glue" that keeps activities from degenerating into disorder.

The Schwerpunkt can also be understood as the harmonizing element or medium through which the contracts of the intent and the mission are realized. It pulls together the efforts of all subordinates and guides them toward the goal, toward the result their commander wants.

3. Surfaces and gaps. Where should you place your Schwerpunkt? The third "filter," surfaces and gaps, helps guide this decision. Quite simply, surfaces and gaps are enemy strengths and weaknesses. Why not just call them that? The term "surfaces and gaps" is useful to the small unit commander, because it describes the kinds of strengths and weaknesses he will often find. A "surface" is a line of enemy defenses. A "gap" is a hole in that line. You want to put your Schwerpunkt opposite a gap, not a surface. In maneuver warfare, you always try to avoid the enemy's strength and hurl your strength against his weaknesses. You want to use judo, not fight a boxing match.

For a platoon, company or even battalion commander, an enemy weakness is likely to be a physical gap in the enemy's position. How can he find the gap? Through what we call "reconnaissance-pull" or "recon-pull."

Currently, most Marine units use the opposite of recon-pull tactics, called "command push." The axis of advance is chosen before the operation begins, and it is seldom altered. The commander pushes however many forces are needed down that axis to make the attack successful. Of course, this often results in throwing strength against strength. With recon-pull, the axis of advance is determined by the results of reconnaissance rather than being fixed by command from above, and it shifts in response to what the recon finds.

An example of one type of attack may be helpful in understanding this. Your forward element is a reconnaissance screen. Its job is to look for surfaces and gaps. When it finds a gap, it goes through, and calls other forces to follow. If the gap seems to be promising, the unit commander commits more forces through it. Some of the forces widen the gap and roll out behind the enemy position that has been penetrated, collapsing it from the rear. Meanwhile, the reconnaissance screen continues to move

forward, always seeking the paths of least resistance. The recon
pulls the main force around the enemy surfaces and ever more
deeply into the enemy position.

Recon-pull requires a different type of reconaissance from
what Marines are used to. Today, most recon forces are committed
deep, along the axis of advance chosen for the "command push."
There is no reconnaissance screen. For recon-pull, you must have
a recon screen. It is different from a security screen, in that
it orients on the enemy, not on your own unit. It must be strong.
Indeed, all your forward forces must be part of it. In maneuver
warfare, recon is everyone's responsibility.

The three "filters" -- mission-type orders, Schwerpunkt, and
surfaces and gaps -- are so important in maneuver warfare that
they form part of our definition of maneuver tactics. But there
are also some other helpful tools. First among them is
firepower.

Firepower is very important in maneuver warfare. Some people
have accused maneuver warfare advocates of downgrading the
importance of firepower. Nothing could be further from the truth.
What changes in maneuver warfare is not the importance of
firepower, but the purposes for which it is used.

Firepower/attrition warfare uses firepower mostly the way the
term implies, to reduce enemy numbers through attrition. Movement
serves firepower; you move to get into a better firing position to
cause more attrition.

Maneuver warfare uses both firepower and movement in a
maneuver context. What does this mean? Usually, you are moving
not just to a better firing position, but to create a series of
unexpected and dangerous situations for the enemy. Only this kind
of movement qualifies as maneuver. The main role of firepower is
to help you maneuver. Firepower is used most often to suppress
the enemy while you move around or through him.

A good example of the use of firepower in maneuver warfare is
given to us by Rommel. At one point during the battle of
Caporetto in 1917, he decided to attack an Italian force on Kuk
mountain. Rommel described the action in his book, Infantry
Attacks:

> He (the Italians) was to be given as little time as
> possible for digging in, for it would be increasingly
> difficult to dislodge him if he were permitted to anchor
> himself firmly. It was essential to use the time for thorough
> preparation of the planned attack.
> In order to maintain surprise I refrained from hampering
> his entrenchment with fire . . . I explained my plan of attack
> against Kuk to Captain Meyr, the General Staff Officer of the
> Alpine Corps, and requested the support of two heavy batteries
> for the attack. My request was granted . . . Now it was
> necessary to prepare the infantry fire support. For this
> purpose I emplaced the light machine guns of the 2nd Company
> and the whole 1st Machine Gun Company on the north and south
> slopes of Hill 1192. Their positions were concealed from the
> enemy on Kuk. I planned to use weak assault teams in the

attack and the automatic weapons had the mission of pinning down the enemy force on Kuk. Targets were designated for each gun.

By 1100 the whole fire detachment (six light machine guns, 2nd Company and 1st Machine Gun Company) under Lieutenant Ludwig, was in concealed position on the north and south slopes of Hill 1192 ready to open fire on the Kuk garrison. An assault team of the 2nd Company consisting of two squads, was in position on the north slope of Hill 1192 and an assault team of the 3rd Company, of equal strength, was on the south slope ready to advance. As soon as firing commenced, the task of these assault squads was to take the saddle between Kuk and Hill 1192, and then, under strong support from artillery and machine guns, to advance against the Kuk garrison along the position on the north slope or through the draw on the southeast slope. I wanted to feel out the hostile position with these assault teams. The 3rd and 4th Rifle Companies and 2nd and 3rd Machine-Gun Companies were in concealed reserve positions in the saddle just east of Hill 1192. I intended to commit them on the north or south slope depending on the success of the initial assault teams.

In his comments on this action, Rommel notes, "The (Rommel) detachment first attacked only with two assault teams of 16 men under the fire support of one machine-gun company, six light machine guns and two heavy batteries. These teams felt out the possibilities of approaching the enemy and I then used the main body to encircle the entire Kuk garrison."[7]

Certainly the amount of firepower Rommel used was substantial, even by current Marine Corps standards. But the purpose was not to bombard the enemy to pieces. Rather, it was to permit movement -- the attack of the assault units --and maneuver -- the encirclement of the entire enemy force.

Just as the purpose of firepower changes in maneuver warfare, so does the way it is employed. Maneuver warfare practitioners strive to employ their fire support systems not just as supporting arms, but as combined arms.

What is the difference? Combined arms hits the enemy with two or more arms simultaneously in such a manner that the actions he must take to defend himself from one make him more vulnerable to another. In contrast, supporting arms is hitting the enemy with two or more arms in sequence, or if simultaneously, then in such combination that the actions the enemy must take to defend himself from one also defends him from the other(s).

Combined arms, like other elements of maneuver warfare, seeks to strike at the enemy psychologically as well as physically. It puts the enemy on the horns of a dilemma. For example, let us say you are defending against an enemy tank attack. You lay a surface minefield with FASCAM to cover an approach that is also within good range of your TOWs. The enemy encounters the mines and the TOWs simultaneously. To avoid the mines, he must move slowly and carefully and keep visibility clear. To avoid the TOWs, he must move quickly and abruptly and obscure visibility. Either choice gets him in trouble, and the fact that his problem has no solution strikes at his mental cohesion.

Supporting arms, in contrast, just faces the enemy with a problem, not a dilemma. Let us say you are facing enemy infantry in entrenchments. You call in an air strike, followed by artillery. To avoid the air, the enemy stays down in his trenches. To avoid the artillery, he does the same. Even if the air and the artillery hit at the same time, he faces no dilemma. His problem has a solution, and the only effect of your action is some attrition.

The distinction between combined arms and supporting arms is important, because combined arms take no more firepower, but will usually be much more effective. If you are fighting outnumbered, you need to get the greatest possible effect from your fire support systems. While circumstances will sometimes compel you to adopt the supporting arms approach, you should always strive for combined arms.

The importance of firepower in maneuver warfare cannot be overemphasized. In some cases, you can find a hole in the enemy's position and infiltrate through. But in many situations, you will have to move in the face of the enemy. The only way to do so is to plaster him with fire, to suppress him while you move around him or through him. The suppression must be very heavy and well-timed to be effective. It is no less heavy or well-timed than in the style of warfare Marines are now accustomed to. The difference is in what you are trying to do with it.

A second important tool in maneuver warfare is the counter-attack. A counterattack is an attack on the enemy's attack. But it is really more than that. It is an action you take after the enemy has irrevocably committed himself.

When the enemy has launched his attack, he has committed himself to a definite action with all or almost all his resources. His momentum is carrying him in a certain direction. If an unexpected threat suddenly presents itself, he will have great difficulty in dealing with it -- much greater difficulty than if he were doing nothing. Again, maneuver warfare is like judo -- you want to use the enemy's own momentum against him. That is what a good counterattack does.

In many instances, the counter-attack will be the key to a successful defense. If you are fighting outnumbered, you will generally not be able to afford a linear defense, a defense where you try to hold a line against the strongest attack your opponent can muster. Even if you hold him, he will have battered you badly. As the smaller force, you can't win by attrition, but you can certainly lose by it!

In the defense as in the offense, you want to shatter the cohesion of the enemy's units, not just kill his troops and destroy his equipment. A common tool for achieving this is the counterattack. In general, the counterattack must have three characteristics to be successful. First, it must be strong. As Guderian often exclaimed, "clobber them, don't jab at them."[8] Second, the counterattack must achieve surprise by striking the advancing enemy at a weak point created by his own forward momentum. Last, and most critical, the success of a counterattack depends upon timing. The commander must be able to sense that point when the enemy, exposed and tiring, is incapable of rapid response to an unexpected threat. Given these three elements, a counterattack can be a devastating tactical tool. To see how devastating, you need only examine the crushing defeats suffered by advancing Russian forces early in 1943, defeats dealt by numerically inferior German forces.

A third important tool, closely related to the counterattack, is the reserve. In both the offense and the defense, a strong reserve provides the key to retaining the initiative and achieving victory. It is a tool with which you can widen gaps and create breakthroughs by reinforcing local successes. It also comprises the counterattack forces. Without a strong reserve, even the most promising opportunities will be wasted, for you will be unable to exploit them. Indeed, a strong reserve offers such potential advantages that it should reflect a sort of inverse proportionality - the weaker the main force with respect to the enemy, the stronger the reserve. Also, the more uncertain or confusing the situation is, the stronger the reserve should be.

Fourth, to be able to outfight the enemy using maneuver warfare, you need a command and control system based on leadership and monitoring. Leadership is something Marines understand well. The antithesis of "micromanagement," it requires each level to take risks and assume responsibility by giving subordinates adequate freedom.

The difference between responsibility and accountability is very important. Responsibility grants wide latitude to subordinates and allows for honest mistakes. Accountability, with its suggestion of punishment, demands absolute knowledge of all subordinates' actions.

The second element of maneuver warfare command and control is monitoring. Simply stated, monitoring supports leadership by providing discreet, by exception, control through observation and listening. Rather than requiring masses of periodic reports, monitoring incorporates forward command principles and "silence is consent" radio monitoring to remain abreast of the tactical situation. Allowing subordinates to fight the battle, the commander intevenes only to exploit opportunities or shift the Schwerpunkt. Closely related to leadership, monitoring allows for maximum information without interference with subordinates.

Both leadership and monitoring are valueless without trust. The "contracts" discussed earlier of intent and mission express that trust - trust by the commander that his subordinates will understand and carry out his desires and trust by those subordinates that they will be supported when exercising their initiative. Such trust is molded by a shared way of thinking. While the specific thoughts and intended actions of adjacent and subordinate commanders will probably be unknown, their thought process must be clearly understood. All levels have to share a comprehension of the intent, the mission, and the focus of effort as well as what each of these means. With this, each Marine can be trusted to act appropriately to defeat the enemy without having to waste critical time requesting permission to take action or subsequently reporting the details.

While sounding almost too simple to be effective, command and control based on trust has been an integral part of modern warfare. It is the way the German Army operated in World War II. To a lesser degree, so does the Bundeswehr today. A Marine officer who was umpiring a Bold Guard exercise was sent to a German brigade headquarters. He asked where the German battalions were so the Marines could assess the effects of their artillery fire. The German brigade commander answered, "How should I know?" The Marine was shocked. He had been told the Germans were good, and this brigade commander not only didn't have his battalions under positive control, he wasn't worried about it! Of course, what he had encountered was the "trust tactics" of maneuver warfare. The brigade commander and the battalion commanders knew how each other thought. When the battalions did something or found something out that the brigade commander needed to know about, they would tell him. Until then, they knew his intent, had their missions, and knew which unit was the Schwerpunkt. That was enough.

A Marine officer rightly said in a recent discussion, "Maneuver warfare tactics are trust tactics. That is their single most important characteristic. And that's the biggest difference from what we do now." It is certainly the biggest change from the current command and control system. Trust and a shared way of thinking, leadership and monitoring, not fancy new C^2 equipment, are what you need to be able to fight using maneuver warfare.

What do all these pictures, definitions, "filters," and tools add up to? Together, they comprise maneuver warfare tactics. You have probably noted a lack of "how to" instructions to this point. While some technical and tactical suggestions will be offered in the next chapter, the essence of maneuver warfare is its approach to tactics and operations. Rather than concentrating on formulas and checklists - with their inherent predictability - maneuver warfare emphasizes a thought process. It is a process of seeing your options, creating new options, and shifting rapidly among those options as the situation changes. Ultimately tactics in maneuver warfare require that you "out-Boyd Cycle" the enemy.

One final, although critical element of maneuver warfare must be discussed: the operational art. To gain an appreciation of this concept, another picture may be helpful. On Tuesday, May 14, 1940, General Heinz Guderian with a corps of three Panzer divisions had just crossed the river Meuse at Sedan. Strong French forces were immediately to his south, threatening his only bridgehead. Len Deighton writes in his book Blitzkrieg:

> Guderian now had to make a decision of such vital importance that it was more a strategic than a tactical one. His three armored divisions had ripped a large gap in the French defenses. To what extent should he consolidate and guard that crossing place? Should he fight the big reserves, which anyone could guess must be moving northward to the gap? Should he batter at the broken edges of the armies on his flanks and thus 'roll up' those defenders? Guderian did none of these things. He paused only to make sure the somewhat mauled Grossdeutschland Regiment and 10. Pz. Div. were in

possession of the high ground at Stonne, a few miles due south
of his crossing place. Guderian took 1 Pz. Div. and 2. Pz.
Div., and disregarding all the theories of war, moved due
west, away from the battle areas, across the flat open land of
the Aisne and the Somme. [9]

What is the operational art? Broadly, it is the art of
winning campaigns. It fits between tactics -- the art of winning
battles -- and strategy -- the art of winning wars. If we think
of operations as the art of the campaign, that tells us what it
is, but not much more. Can we come up with a more useful
definition?

The operational art is the art of using tactical events --
battles or refusals to give battle - to strike directly at the
enemy's strategic center of gravity. For the commander, it is the
art of deciding where and when to fight on the basis of the
strategic plan. You can see this definition in Guderian's decision
at Sedan. Guderian looked beyond his immediate tactical situation
to see that a victory against the French to his south meant
nothing, while a successful advance to the west meant everything.
He linked his tactical to his strategic situation in such a way as
to see what future tactical actions he should take. He used the
tactical event -- the crossing of the Meuse --strategically, and
decided what tactical actions to take -- where to fight and
whether to fight -- on a strategic basis.

Why is the operational art important if you are to do maneuver
warfare? Because it is through excellence in the operational art
more than through maneuver in tactical battle (as important as
that is) that a smaller force can defeat a larger one.
Traditionally, American armies have tried to attain their
strategic objectives by accumulating tactical victories. They
have given battle where and whenever it has been offered, wearing
their enemy down engagement after engagement. This is attrition
warfare on the operational level. Even if each battle is fought
according to maneuver principles, operational attrition warfare is
inappropriate for the smaller force, because even the best-fought
battle brings some casualties. Fighting this way, a smaller force
can win battle after battle, only to find itself facing yet
another battle, but with no force left to fight it.

The small force wins only by using battle sparingly, by giving
battle only where and when a victory will strike directly at the
enemy's strategic center of gravity. Determining when and where
to fight so a tactical victory has a strategic result is the
operational art. If the Marine Corps is to do maneuver warfare,
it must have MAB and MAF commanders who are expert in this art.
The first steps toward this are to recognize the operational level
in doctrine (as the Army has in the new FM 100-5), to begin
teaching it in the schools at Quantico (especially through
historical case studies), and to incorporate it in the planning
for campaigns, both in CPXs and in actual situations such as the
defense of Norway. Unless we develop excellence at the
operational as well as the tactical level, we will continue to
fight attrition warfare.

3
Techniques and Organization[1]

While maneuver warfare cannot be done by formula, some formulas may be helpful in doing it. As already noted, techniques are formulas, and they are very important in maneuver warfare. Organization is also done by formula, at least to some extent.

Many of the techniques taught in FMFMs, Operational Handbooks, and Marine Corps schools will carry over into maneuver warfare. In fact, the Marine Corps' main weakness in techniques is not that most of its current techniques are wrong or outdated, but that it doesn't know how to do them very well. It cannot be said often enough that excellence in techniques is vitally important in maneuver warfare. Marines must improve their performance in techniques if maneuver warfare is ever going to mean anything beyond the confines of the schools and the pages of the Gazette.

But at the same time, maneuver warfare does suggest some new techniques and also some new approaches to how Marines organize. It may be helpful to look at some different types of units and functions and see what some of the changes might be.

The Rifle Squad

Although combat experience should indicate otherwise, the rifle squad currently occupies a relatively minor place in Marine Corps tactical thought. Squad level training and doctrine seem to suggest that the squad has little independent tactical value. The squad has been relegated to the role of a subunit whose movements are closely controlled by the platoon commander.

Considered in terms of maneuver warfare, this attitude is disastrous. Because it is often at the point of contact, the squad must be able to react rapidly to changing situations and to seek out enemy weaknesses. This initiative, for which the German Stosstruppen became famous, demands that the squad assume a primary tactical role and that its organization and training be based on more than movement formations.

The basic structure of the rifle squad should be simple and should reflect the level of initiative expected. Rather than having two symmetrical teams, as exist now, the squad should be organized into a probing team and a support team. The probing team, composed of riflemen and grenadiers, should act as the

25

probing, breeching, and, where necessary, assault element. The support team, armed with the squad automatic weapon and grenade launchers, should provide the firepower to suppress enemy opposition.

Although for administrative purposes the squad may have a set structure (see Figure 1), the squad leader should task organize his squad according to the situation. For example, if moving through wooded terrain and uncertain of enemy locations, the squad leader might opt to place only the team leader, a rifleman, and a grenadier in the probing team, reserving the bulk of his strength to exploit the situation as it develops. If reinforced with an anti-tank missile team or a machine gun, the squad leader might again realign his squad, while retaining the functional team structure. The simplicity of this organization allows the squad leader to react to changing situations without seeking higher level support and approval.

Some of the techniques employed by a squad organized this way will differ from those currently in use. Most significant, only one basic formation will be needed - the overwatch column. Much like the squad formation employed by the Army for the past decade, the overwatch column places the probing team forward and the support team to the rear. Distances between the two vary depending upon the situation. Individuals within the teams will be positioned by the team leader to meet tactical requirements.

The overwatch column contrasts sharply with existing doctrine, which has the squad shifting through many complex formations attempting to adjust to changing circumstances.[2] The advantage lies in the simplicity of the formation, which enables the squad leader to concentrate on fighting the enemy rather than controlling the gyrations of his squad. The teams, specifically organized as fire and maneuver elements, will require minimal control during those crucial initial seconds under fire.

While dividing the squad into two task-oriented teams would appear to separate fire and maneuver, the opposite is in fact true. Each team, organized and trained for specific tasks, will quickly come to rely on the other for tactical success. The probing team, being more lightly armed, will search for an exploitable weakness or present the enemy with an immediate, close range threat. The support team, keyed to the movements of the probing team, will position its suppressive fire, either by rapidly shifting fires or by physical displacement, so as to present the enemy with a longer range, equally dangerous threat. Individually, the two teams present easily counterable menaces; together, they become a combined arms team requiring the enemy to expose himself to one in order to combat the other.[3]

The concept of combined arms can be expanded to the platoon and company level, with one important change. In addition to forming probing -- or at the platoon and company level, penetrating -- and support elements, the commander also must form an exploitation element. While this may sound like current doctrine, which calls for a maneuver element, a base of fire, and a reserve, it is conceptually quite different. The penetrating element should be as small as possible, seldom more than a reinforced squad. Its mission is breaching the enemy defense.

11-MAN RIFLE SQUAD

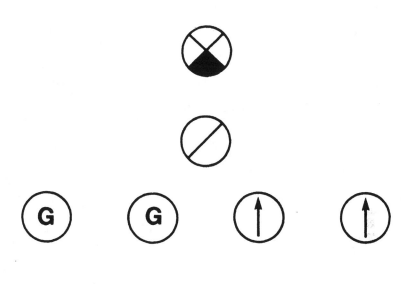

SUPPORT TEAM

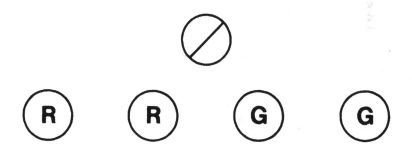

PROBING TEAM

Figure 1

Once it has found or created a gap, the exploitation element, containing the bulk of the unit, should push through and expand both laterally and in depth to destroy the enemy position from the rear. The support element, having suppressed the enemy so the penetrating and exploitation elements could succeed, then shifts its fires forward and to the flanks, supporting the exploitation and enabling the penetrating element to resume probing. At the platoon level this process of probing, penetrating and exploiting will generally be carried out on a single axis. At the company level, two or three separate penetrating elements may advance simultaneously, with the commander commiting his exploitation element where the penetrating element has the greatest success.

This technique requires decentralization of control. Penetrating elements advance semi-independently, their actions guided by their missions, with control measures limited to zones of action and, sometimes (but not often), limits of advance. Squad leadership demands initiative and boldness. The platoon and company commanders, rather than attempting to control squad movement, make the critical timing decisions on when to commit the exploitation element or, at the company level, shift the Schwerpunkt from one penetrating element to another.

To enable all three elements to carry out their missions, task organization is essential. Penetrating elements, particularly those facing prepared positions, may need combat engineer, machine gun, or light mortar support to provide immediate suppression. Exploitation elements may need anti-tank teams, mortars and artillery. Most situations will entail cross-attachment, dedicated fire support (to include aviation), and minimal, by-exception control measures. In no other way will small unit leaders be able to create and capitalize on momentary enemy weaknesses.

The Infantry Battalion and Higher Levels

The battalion and higher level commander's time and attention should be devoted mostly to tactics and the operational art rather than techniques. His primary tasks are deciding whether to give or refuse battle, conceptualizing the battle, giving initial orders that support his concept, and then seizing and capitalizing on opportunities created by subordinate units. Rather than directing all the movements of his companies through detailed control measures and requirements for constant situation reports, the battalion commander makes the critical timing decisions that enable forward elements to exploit promising opportunities. He must be able to assess developing situations rapidly and see through confusion to seize opportunities without becoming enmeshed in details. Control measures must be minimal and designed for guidance rather than explicit regulation of maneuver elements. Thus, a company commander seeing an opportunity in another company's zone of action should not hesitate to cross a boundary to exploit it.

Two techniques are useful to battalion and higher level commanders: command from the front and mission-type orders. Few

commanders can adequately assess a situation and take prompt
action in response to events while remaining at their command
posts. Battlefield reports, however often submitted, lack
timeliness and are often exaggerated or, worse, inaccurate. They
usually result in requirements for more reports as commanders
attempt to develop an accurate picture. The result is a slow OODA
loop, with events outpacing reactions.

This problem can often be solved by a commander who, leaving
more routine matters of coordination and logistics to his staff,
positions himself where he can see and directly influence the
battle at the Schwerpunkt. A close corollary can be found between
Israeli military success and casualties among leaders, all of whom
are imbued with the idea of command from the front. To Marines
this means that even the mobile CP created from the assault
amphibian command vehicle may be too cumbersome. Something as
simple as a jeep carrying a secure voice radio may be far more
effective. With it, the commander, accompanied by a few crucial
members of his staff, may concentrate his efforts on tactics and
the operational art. The rest of his staff, more centrally
located and following behind, can see to the techniques.

The mission-type order helps the battalion and higher level
commander focus on tactics rather than techniques. As discussed
in an earlier chapter, the heart of the mission-type order is the
commander's intent. Through it, he expresses his
conceptualization of the battle and maintains tactical control of
his subordinates.

In contrast to the current 5-paragraph order, in which the
mission is usually to seize a piece of terrain, the mission-type
order provides subordinate commanders with the an understanding of
what their superior wants to accomplish vis-a-vis the enemy. For
example, paragraph two of the five paragraph order states, usually
in geographic terms, the mission of the unit. It may read
something like, "At 0900 on 1 Jan 8_, this battalion will attack
and seize Hill 48 (Grid 123456) and be prepared to continue the
attack on order." The mission-type order would, instead, state,
"At 0900 on 1 Jan 8_, this battalion will attack through Hill 48
in order to prevent enemy observation and interference with
amphibious offloading in the beachhead area." This order clearly
shows the intent of the commander and orients on the enemy rather
than a terrain feature. Subordinate commanders, aware of the
overall purpose of the attack, may deviate from the geographic
objective in order to accomplish the commander's intent. The
requirement to attack through Hill 48 also allows them to exploit
any gaps created by the attack. If necessary, instructions in
paragraph 3 - Execution - can delineate limits of advance. While
a quick comparison of the format of the five-paragraph order and
the mission type order shows little difference (see Figure 2),
closer examination reveals conceptual changes that shift the focus
towards more flexible, yet still controlled tactics.

Mission-type orders and forward command may force
reexamination of many current techniques of command and control.
As has already been mentioned, reliance on detailed reporting,
particularly when cued to time schedules, cannot keep pace with
the rapid decision cycle envisioned in maneuver warfare. Instead,

reporting by exception, with subordinate units reporting
noteworthy successes or failures, offers greater flexibility and
more rapid local decision-making. The commander's mobile CP,
travelling with the forward units, may only include his operations
officer and his Fire Support Controller, each equipped with a
direct link to the main command post. If the commander loses
contact with the main CP, then the executive officer steps in to
assume command. Likewise, if a situation should arise in which a
critical decision must be made and time prevents consultation with
the commander, the executive officer is empowered to act. Rapid
response, based on mutual understanding of intent, must always
override considerations of prerogative.

Figure 2 Comparison of Five-Paragraph and Mission-Type Orders

5-Paragraph Order	Mission-Type Order

1. Situation
  a. Enemy Forces
  b. Friendly Forces
  c. Attachments/Detachments
  d. Commander's Evaluation
    (optional)
	1. Situation
	  a. Enemy Forces
	  b. Friendly Forces
	  c. Attachments/Detachments
	  d. Commander's Intent
	    (required) A clear
	    statement of what the
	    commander wants to
	    accomplish. The intent
	    two levels up should be
	    included.

2. Mission. A statement of the
   issuing unit's mission,
   usually emphasizing seizure
   of terrain objectives.
	2. Mission. A clear statement
	   of what the unit is to do,
	   usually defined in terms of
	   the enemy, not terrain.

3. Execution
  a. Concept of operations.
    Summary of scheme of
    maneuver and fire
    support plan.
 	
  b. Subordinate missions.
    Usually given in terms
    of terrain.
 	
  c. Coordinating instruc-
    tions.
	3. Execution
	  a. Concept of operations.
	    Designation of focus of
	    main effort (<u>Schwerpunkt</u>),
	    initial axis of advance,
	    and any limiting instruc-
	    tions.
	  b. Subordinate missions.
	    Usually given in terms of
	    the enemy rather than
	    terrain.
	  c. Coordinating instruc-
	    tions.

4. Service Support	4. Service Support

5. Command and Signal
  a. Signal instructions
  b. Command posts, location
    of commander.
	5. Command and Signal
	  a. Signal instructions
	  b. Command posts, location
	    of commander.

Fire Support

Fire support is worthless if it is not timely. Weight of ordnance is less important than _rapid_ effect on target. Tank gunners and infantrymen have understood this for decades.

The ultimate uselessness of the massive volumes of shells slowly poured on Ypres, Iwo Jima, Okinawa and the jungles of Vietnam should have taught artillerymen and pilots the same thing. Yet the newly procured M198 howitzer, an 8-ton behemoth, lumbers slowly about the battlefield, widening the gap between advancing maneuver elements and their fire support. Close air support, fearful of modern air-defense weapons, has come to rely more on preplanned missions, the time-consuming coordination of which restricts availability of immediate air support. Like the French earlier in this century, the Marine Corps seems to be adopting the idea that firepower conquers and infantry occupies. Fire support coordination increasingly seems to drive infantry and tank tactics, when it should be the other way around.

Maneuver warfare will require new fire support techniques, techniques that ensure timeliness. Tactics, particularly recon-pull tactics, demand immediate suppressive fire support. The advancing assault and exploitation elements must have rapidly available suppressive fires.

One possible technique for providing them is the use of dedicated aircraft and batteries. While dedicating fire support assets to specific companies or battalions may reduce the ability to mass and shift fires, the benefits may often outweigh the loss. The vertical take-off and landing capabilities of the AV-8 and the attack helicopter make these aircraft ideal for dedicated tasking. Co-located with the ground commander, their pilots will be attuned to the ground situation and the aircraft will be immediately available. Their bombs and rockets, while of limited volume, can be timely. Dedicated artillery batteries, perhaps operating in the split-battery mode, can also offer timely fire support. Readily responsive to a single ground commander, the dedicated battery should be able to place immediate fires on enemy positions.

Dedicating aircraft and batteries will not always be an appropriate technique. Heavy reliance on dedicated aircraft or batteries degrades the total effectiveness of Marine Corps supporting arms. Deciding when and how much to dedicate remains a primary responsibility of the MAGTF commander. A careful balance is necessary between decentralization to provide immediate suppression and more centralized control to mass fires and rapidly shift fire support.

Even when control of fire support assets is centralized, target selection and engagement should generally not be. Through the mission-type order and, especially, designation of the Schwerpunkt, priority of fires is automatically established. Specific selection of targets should then be left to forward commanders. Higher level fire support coordination centers should generally restrict themselves to allocating assets to maneuvering forces and ensuring that adequate fire support continues.

Fire support thus takes on a dual character. Centralized control of fire support, through the use of general support missions, remains essential for initial prep fires in support of the Schwerpunkt and to provide rapid shifting of fires to support sudden changes in the battle. Equally essential, however, are the immediately available suppressive fires provided by direct support and dedicated fire support assets. Demanding little time for coordination or preplanning, this category of fire support becomes an integral part of the maneuver forces, enabling them to act and react swiftly in response to changing battlefield conditions.

Tanks and Mechanized Infantry

The last ten years have seen substantial changes in the way Marines view tanks and Amtracks. A decade ago, tanks were almost always seen clanking along at two miles per hour with infantry walking alongside, just as in World War I. The tank was not really a tank, but a combination assault gun and anti-tank cannon. In both roles, it was strictly an infantry support weapon. Amtracks were a device for getting ashore, after which they waited for the dismounted infantry to win the battle and come back to claim them.

Today, things are very different in most Marine divisions and exercises. Marines no longer think of "the tank," but instead of "the tank battalion." The tank battalion is seen as a maneuver unit. In most cases, it is kept together and used for a decisive stroke. Often it is reinforced by a battalion of mechanized infantry, mounted in Amtracks. In relatively open terrain, even a two-battalion armor/mech battle group can have a powerful effect on the enemy, especially if it is used to launch a surprise attack or counterattack.

This new organization of armor and mech assets is consistent with maneuver warfare. As with everything else, how it is task organized and employed depends on the situation; there will probably even be situations where it is appropriate to distribute armor assets to the infantry. But for tanks and tracks, maneuver warfare is likely to mean more of what they are already doing: practicing to work as highly mobile combined arms teams.

However, new ideas are still needed in the Marine tank/mech community. Tanks and Amtracks will soon be joined by a third element: the Light Armored Vehicle (LAV) battalions. How should the LAVs be organized and employed? Answers to those questions must wait on substantial experimentation in the field. But a few observations might be helpful.

First, it must always be kept in mind that LAVs are tactically very fragile. Their armor is very light, and only the assault gun variant will have any anti-tank capability. If LAVs are misused, they can easily become coffins for their crews. They must never be thrown against prepared defenses, and if they fight tanks they must do so from ambush.

Second, despite LAVs' tactical fragility, the LAV battalion should be regarded as a general purpose force. It would be a mistake to say, "The LAV battalion is to be employed for reconnaisance and security," or something similar. It should be employed according to the situation, not so as to conform to a list of specific missions. One of the reasons the German Panzer divisions were so much more effective than their French equivalents, the DLMs and DCRs, is that the Germans regarded the Panzers as general purpose, to be used according to the situation, while the French doctrine specified set tasks for their armored divisions.

Third, the LAV battalion should generally be committed as a battalion. If LAVs are distributed in penny packets, a few to each infantry battalion, their presence on the battlefield will not even be felt. Just as the Marine Corps has learned to think of tank battalions, not individual tanks, so it must think of the LAV battalion as the basic combat element.

Fourth, if the LAV battalion is to have enough options available to it to be effective, it must have a combined arms capability. This means that an assault gun variant must be procured -- something that now appears to be in question. A TOW variant is no substitute; when you suddenly spot an enemy tank a few hundred meters away, the TOW reacts too slowly to keep you alive. If the assault gun variant is not bought, the LAV battalion will be little more than a battalion of motorized infantry.

Fifth, both doctrine development and subsequent employment should focus on the operational more than the tactical level. This was the secret of the Panzers' success: they were used best when, instead of just fighting battles, they struck directly at an enemy's strategic center of gravity, such as the juncture of the French armies in Belgium with those in France itself. A good first sentence in the LAV doctrinal manual might be, "The LAV battalion is an operational, not a tactical weapon; it will assume only those tactical tasks which are operationally significant."

Sixth and finally, in developing its LAV doctrine, the Marine Corps should seek to learn from others. The French have been the world's leaders in LAVs, and their thoughts and observations might be very valuable, especially those they have grounded on the combat experience of nations to whom they have sold their vehicles. Brazilian LAVs have also been used in combat, including in the Middle East, and the Brazilians might have some useful ideas. So might the South Africans. Too often, Americans do not pay much attention to what others are doing and learning. In the case of the LAV, where other nations have had such vehicles in service for decades, this could be a costly mistake.

Engineers

Engineers have been very important in maneuver warfare. In World War II, German engineers (pioneers) were often the lead elements in an attack, because their understanding of terrain was very helpful in guiding the recon-pull advance. If you ask an Israeli officer today what his most important piece of equipment is, he will often answer, "the bulldozer." The bulldozer is the first servant of the Israeli tanks, both in preparing hasty defenses and in clearing routes of advance. The Soviets often say that almost any natural obstacle is a lesser hindrance to an advance than a prepared, manned defense, which suggests engineers are likely to be found at the tip of their <u>Schwerpunkt</u>.

What does all this mean for Marine engineers? The best answer is, "Ask your friendly local engineer." Many Marine engineers have been doing alot of thinking about what maneuver warfare means for them. But too often, nobody bothers to ask them. Engineers are not seen as part of the combined arms force, even though they are a very important part. In exercises, they are left in the rear to play with their own equipment, instead of being pushed to the forefront where they will be needed in combat.

The first step in adapting Marine engineers to maneuver warfare is to open the door and invite them in when you are doing your planning, thinking about your tactics in a given situation, and, for those in Headquarters, drawing up your budgets. They are as much a part of your team as infantry, tanks or artillery.

Combat Service Support

Before concluding this chapter, one additional area must be discussed: combat service support. Although vital to combat success, combat service support has been relegated by many Marines to the world of narrow specialists, where it is presumed that the mysteries of maintenance, supply, and transport will be solved. This attitude has led to a combat logistics system that more resembles a catalog sales department than an integral element of a combined arms team. While in theory the MAGTF concept calls for responsive logistics support, reality is too often otherwise. Pack-laden Marines, more resembling mules than fighting men, are combined with a system of requisitions and centralized resupply and maintenance that often seems more responsive to logisticians' desires for orderliness than combat requirements for immediate support.

Combat service support, to be truly effective, cannot be separated from tactics and operations. Just as with fire support, combat service support must be immediately available to the forward commander. Such responsiveness can only be provided by using forward-push logistics. Developed initially by the Wehrmacht as part of its <u>Blitzkrieg</u> doctrine and adapted by the Israelis, forward push logistics lays the burden of combat service support on logisticians rather than combat units.

The heart of forward-push logistics is the ability of combat service support elements to anticipate the logistics needs of forward units. Rather than waiting for requests, which invariably involve delays in transmission and response, each level of command anticipates requirements and pushes forward whatever is likely to be needed. An excellent example of forward push logistics is the combat service support envisioned for Marine Mechanized Combined Arms Task Forces. Each echelon replenishes the combat service support element at the next subordinate level, beginning with the Combat Service Support Detachment, moving to the Mobile Combat Service Support Detachment, and on to the regimental, battalion, and company trains. Combat unit replenishment is conducted during momentary lulls in fighting.[4] Using a combination of supply personnel and good judgement by

logistics officers, subordinate units' needs can be readily
anticipated and provided for in advance. Such a system, highly
flexible and geared towards the tactical and operational
requirements of the battlefield, will enable combat units to
continue fighting unburdened by constant requirements to
requisition and resupply.

Conclusion

The ideas in this chapter are offered as an appetizer, not a
full meal. Much additional work needs to be done on techniques
and organization for maneuver warfare. No one is as well
qualified to do it as Marines. Read again your FMFMs and
Operational Handbooks, this time with an eye on maneuver warfare,
and see what is still applicable (a great deal will be). Work
with your neighboring infantry, tanks, tracks, artillery and
engineers. Bring the air wing into the discussions, especially at
the schools. See what techniques jump out at you from historical
case studies.

Theorists outside the Marine Corps can suggest some basic
ideas about maneuver warfare. But translating the ideas into
practice takes people with combat experience, with opportunities
to test ideas in the field, and with direct personal experience
with friction. That means you. If you start asking around, you
will find plenty of fellow Marines who want to join with you in
working the problems.

4
Amphibious Operations[1]

Recent events have provided new evidence to support Marines' long-standing belief in the importance of amphibious operations. Argentina's seizure of the Falkland Islands and Great Britain's response both demonstrated the need for amphibious forces. In the Middle East, Israeli Army units sliced into Lebanon using a combination of armored thrusts and amphibious bounds. The Iran-Iraq war has put new emphasis on America's commitments in the Persian Gulf, commitments that must be backed by a strong amphibious capability.

Yet, at the same time, modern weaponry has raised serious questions about the potential costs of amphibious landings. In the Falklands, heavy casualties jolted the British. Even in its weakness, Argentina shocked military observers by exacting a frightening toll of British shipping; the nearly disastrous landing at Port Fitzroy provided a bloody lesson in the destructiveness of today's weapons. Israeli amphibious forces, mindful of Russian-equipped Palestinians, remained closely tied to advancing inland columns. Today, planners at Central Command are grappling with problems echoing those encountered by the British and Israelis.

The problem of getting forces ashore becomes even more difficult when the presence of mechanized, highly mobile enemy ground forces must be taken into account. Many of the basic conditions for a traditional amphibious assault may no longer be attainable. It may be impossible to isolate amphibious objective areas. Air and naval superiority may be achievable only temporarily. Enemy defenses and counterstrokes may prevent the landing force commander from methodically building up his combat power ashore before breaking out of his beachhead.

Since the early months of 1943, amphibious operation planners have relied on these three basic requirements being met. Current amphibious exercises assume that they have been. Unfortunately, the enemy may not agree with our assumptions. Nor can we expect the problems to be solved by hi-tech "miracle weapons." LCACs and JVX aircraft, if employed in traditional ways, will change nothing. The solution requires far more than the mere application of technology.

36

Does maneuver warfare offer some possible solutions? It may. Today's amphibious doctrine traces its origins to the early years of the Depression, when a few Marines at Quantico produced the first manual on landing operations. Tested and expanded in the late 1930s and proven by combat in World War II, it has remained remarkably effective in the face of changing technology and methods of warfare. Yet, as we have noted, amphibious operations face serious new challenges. To meet them, amphibious doctrine must be capable of combining new ideas with proven principles. Maneuver warfare may offer some of the new ideas necessary for such a doctrinal revitalization.

What are some of the changes maneuver warfare might bring to amphibious landings? The first, and possibly the most important, might be the replacement of landing waves followed by a beachhead build-up with landing points and immediate thrusts deep into the enemy's positions. This would be analogous to the replacement of the linear attack with the reconnaissance-pull advance in infantry tactics.

Instead of the broad landing beaches currently used, much narrower landing points, sometimes no more than ten yards wide, may often offer oportunities to seek out enemy weaknesses. By landing his forces across multiple landing points, a commander would retain the ability to develop situations while committing minimal forces. If successful, initial landing forces could immediately be reinforced by uncommitted units; if not, they could quickly be withdrawn and shifted to reinforce more successful landings.

Such an approach proved highly successful during MacArthur's drive along the New Guinea coast in 1943 and 1944. Hamstrung by limited quantities of amphibious shipping and unsure of Japanese defensive concentrations, the Seventh Amphibious Force became expert at limited visibility landings across lightly defended landing points, rapidly reinforcing successes and evacuating failures. Many of these landings were carried out in the face of enemy air and naval superiority.[2]

Reconnaissance elements would play a crucial role in landing point amphibious assaults, just as they do in other recon-pull attacks. Reconnaissance forces would be tasked with identifying gaps in enemy defenses, both on the coastline and further inland. The landing force commander would be ready to exploit identified enemy weaknesses rapidly by pushing assault forces ashore to reinforce successful reconnaissance elements.

The new LCAC and the JVX could both make big differences in amphibious landings if combined with a landing point assault. The LCAC could well become the primary ingredient in recon-pull amphibious landings. Loaded with exploitation forces, possibly including mechanized task forces of tanks and/or LAVs, LCACs could constitute a highly mobile, seaborne reserve able to reinforce success quickly. The LCAC could also be invaluable for shifting from one landing point to another. One can picture the confusion of an enemy defender, faced with a large number of simultaneous landings, trying to counter an amphibious Schwerpunkt that can be rapidly shifted by sea. Add in high speed, low altitude JVX transports able to carry out similar missions further inland and such landings could prove devastating to the cohesion of enemy coastal defenses.

Many of the tactical ingredients and techniques of infantry and tank/mech ground combat would carry over into landing point, recon-pull amphibious operations. Effective control of forces landing in dispersed points could only be maintained through mission-type orders. Such orders, clearly stating the intent of the overall task force commander as well as the amphibious and landing force commanders, would allow dispersed units to act with the necessary freedom. More important, subordinate commanders would understand what they were to do if required to shift to another landing point or to drive inland. They would be guided by the commander's intent, not geographic objectives, beachhead lines, or limits of advance. While these geographic control measures may, at times, be helpful, they should be guides, not iron shackles.

Just as in other combat situations, the commander should not rely on detailed reports to adjust his focus of main effort or react to rapidly shifting circumstances: instead he should position himself at the Schwerpunkt where he can see the developing situation. Banks of radios aboard ships will not provide the landing force commander with the type of information and control needed to get a 'feel' for the battle. By placing himself well forward, he can assess the situation and allocate forces to influence the action in a decisive way. Marines seized Tarawa largely because Colonel Shoup established a command post ashore and assumed control, directing crucial landings of reinforcements. Inland, subordinate commanders fought the tactical battle, fully understanding the landing force mission. The 2d Marine Division Commander aboard the USS MARYLAND merely watched.[3]

What other changes might maneuver warfare bring to amphibious operations? It certainly might bring into question the current division between the so-called ship-to-shore movement and operations ashore. By tactically separating the naval and the land components, current amphibious doctrine has created a split that could seriously degrade Marines' ability to react to rapidly changing situations. Command relationships have always been recognized as critical in an amphibious assault. They must reflect the fact that an amphibious landing is a single entity. Naval and land forces become interchangeable components of a single whole.

A key factor in determining command relationships should be the operational, not just the tactical, situation. Both naval and ground force commanders must understand the operational goal and be prepared to sacrifice short term tactical goals to achieve it. Whether the amphibious task force or landing force commander controls elements of an amphibious landing should be wholly dependent upon whatever considerations, be they naval or ground, are critical to achieving the operational goal.

Further, in developing the command relationships for an amphibious operation every effort should be made to ensure total integration of all arms. Naval gunfire, Navy and Marine air

support, and artillery, as well as combat and service support
units all require integration to be effective. The ability to
combine diverse elements, quickly shifting them to meet rapidly
changing situations, is essential. This requires task
organization down to the lowest levels. Decentralization of
artillery, naval gunfire, and even aviation assets is particularly
crucial during the initial stages of an amphibious landing.
Unlike in today's situation, task organizations cannot be confined
by service jealousies. It must be possible to put Navy ships
capable of delivering gunfire, air, or anti-air support in direct
support of a Marine landing force. Conversely, Marine forces
ashore may have to be subordinated to a naval command in other
situations. The measure of command must be the ability to
allocate forces at the right time and place to achieve the
objectives. Combined arms synergism cannot be restricted by more
traditional, and too often parochial, tasking of forces.

Because a maneuver warfare amphibious assault will from the
beginning be looking beyond the beach, aviation will need to give
more thought to battlefield air interdiction. Battlefield air
interdiction calls for fixed wing aircraft to attack targets
beyond the Fire Support Coordination Line. Fully briefed on the
ground commander's intent, pilots flying such missions would be
tasked to attack enemy forces beyond the immediate zone of combat.
Command centers, logistics elements, and, most important, mobile
reserves would be important targets for air attack. The resulting
destruction and confusion would degrade the enemy commander's
ability to react to changing conditions in the ground battle.

Fire support for maneuver warfare amphibious landings, like
that for operations ashore, should combine decentralization with
the ability of the landing force commander to exploit success
rapidly. In a multiple landing point amphibious operation, each
assault element must be given control of the artillery, air, and
naval gunfire assets it needs. This approach is already included
in the MAGTF concept. Each assault element commander, however,
must also be ready to support adjacent landing points with fire,
as well as with maneuver. Situations may occur that will call for
control of assets by one assault element commander that were
originally part of another task force.

No amphibious operation will succeed if it is not supported
logistically. For a maneuver warfare landing, the current
logistics doctrine of on-call resupply and gradual buildup in a
Beachhead Support Area is inadequate. The vulnerability of the
beachhead supply base is a particularly serious problem. It is a
"nose" by which the enemy can grab the landing force and compel it
to give battle on unfavorable terms.

Amphibious logistics should, instead, be based on the
principle of forward-push logistics, which provides the commander
with the type of fluid support necessary to fight a maneuver
warfare battle. In an amphibious landing, forward-push logistics
should center on mobile loaded floating dumps and TACLOG groups
with expanded responsibilities. Preloading vehicles with combat
essential supplies and similarly organizing logistics and
maintenance units would largely erase the immediate need for
vulnerable dumps and installations ashore. TACLOG groups, closely

attuned to the situation ashore, would then decide which logistics elements were required ashore and order them to land. Once across the beach, these elements would be pushed forward by the shore party. Upon completion of their logistics mission, the mobile elements would return to amphibious shipping for replenishment and reassignment in floating reserve.

The Marine Corps' new logistics transport vehicle, the 'Dragon Wagon,' offers an excellent means of preloading essential supplies into modules that can be rapidly brought ashore. Additionally, these procedures can be modified to include both helicopter and fixed-wing logistics packets. The concept of mobile logistics is currently undergoing evaluation.[4] Its application in amphibious operations requires that both naval and ground force components, from shipboard crews to forward combat elements, remember that support must anticipate combat needs rather than respond to them.

The amphibious picture presented in this chapter is one of development of time proven amphibious warfare doctrine. Much current doctrine requires no change; indeed, as one Marine recently said, "amphibious warfare is maneuver warfare."[5] The pages of LFM 0-1, Doctrine for Amphibious Operations, require few detailed changes. What is required, however, is an extremely high degree of command flexibility. Decentralized control of widely dispersed landing points through which small, self-contained MAGTF's must be projected and reinforced requires commanders with a keen appreciation of the tactical art. Even more important are the changes required to apply maneuver warfare and amphibious warfare at the operational, rather than the technical or tactical level. The techniques offered in this chapter should be means by which the amphibious operation can be a devastating military tool. Of themselves, techniques and tactics are useless. They must be ensconced in the operational art, which means we must develop commanders who understand that art.

5
Education and Training

It is my great and constant hope that the Marine Corps will produce some outstanding man for the country. Such men are somewhere, and they may as well be in our classes as anywhere else. I do not want such a person to be hammered down by narrowness and dogmas: to have his mind cramped by compulsory details. It is my constant ambition to see the Marine officers filled with ambition, initiative, and originality; and they can get these attributes only by liberality of thought - broad thought - thought that differs from precedent and the compulsory imprint of others.[1]

The above words, written in 1934 by the Commandant of Marine Corps Schools, Brigadier General J. C. Breckinridge, offer a clear assessment of the true value of military education. Written during an era of unparalled Marine Corps innovation, these words are as relevant today as fifty years ago. Indeed, General Breckinridge's concept of military education could well have been developed with maneuver warfare in mind.

Today, the term "education" has become almost meaningless. People speak of a "high school education." They assume any college will automatically "provide an education." Virtually any sort of instruction is assumed to have "educational value." But education is more than the learning of skills or the acquisition of facts. It includes acquiring a broad understanding of one's culture, its development and the principles upon which it is founded. Education develops the ability to put immediate situations into a larger context built of history, philosophy, and an understanding of the nature of man. Inherent in education is the ability to think logically, to approach problem solving methodically, but without a predetermined set of solutions.

Although more specifically focused, military education requires much the same process of development. Thoroughly grounded in the art of war - the soldier's "culture" - an educated officer must understand the guiding concepts of his profession, why they are held to be true, and how they evolved. He must be able to put whatever military situation he faces into a larger context of military history, theory, and men's behavior in combat.

41

The development of an ability to think logically, under the stress of battle, must always be a fundamental objective of military education.

Military education is basic to the definition of maneuver warfare and is an integral component of tactics and the operational art. Without military education, tactics and operations become little more than applied checklists. True education removes the need for checklists and "school solutions," enabling commanders to approach each problem equipped with a large array of possible solutions, placing the problem in a larger context and evolving innovative answers. The common thought process developed in officers through military education binds techniques, tactics and the operational art. As noted earlier, it is also a basis of command and control in maneuver warfare.

Military education, when defined in terms of how rather than what to think, conflicts with current Marine Corps educational concepts. The Marine Corps education system is, in reality, one devoted to techniques. While the argument can be made that, due to long periods of absence from the FMF and increasing complexities of modern combat, officers must be solidly grounded in the technical fundamentals, the relative exclusion of innovative thought is tragic. Despite some historical analysis at AWS and the Command and Staff College aimed at improving decision-making skills, there seems to be little room for questioning and creative thinking. Even more tragically, many officers show little inclination for creativity. Beginning at The Basic School, techniques are memorized with little broad understanding of their conceptual foundations. This emphasis on techniques - the so-called "basics" - has led to stagnancy in Marine Corps education.

How should the schools be reformed? Looking first at TBS, the idea that "we only have enough time to teach the basics" must be abandoned. Instead, lieutenants should first be taught how to think "two levels up," and only afterwards instructed in the techniques and terminology necessary for commanding a platoon. This issue was discussed by Wehrmacht Colonel H. G. Pestke in the October 1983 issue of the Marine Corps Gazette. Colonel Pestke said: "For our officer candidates, we use battalion scenarios. He is not a lieutenant yet, but consistent with our (German) method of training two levels up, we put the candidate in the battalion-level situation first. This way he builds a framework of understanding that will enable him to know what he is doing when he begins considering how to employ his platoon."[2]

The same principle applies to AWS and Command & Staff: captains should be taught to think at the MAB level and majors and lieutenant colonels at the MAF level. Only thus can they develop the understanding they need to lead companies and battalions under a system that relies on mission orders.

Second, TBS should give adequate time and attention to concepts, theory, and history. A lieutenant will not become an expert in theory or history during the 21 weeks he is a student at TBS, but he should be made fully aware of their importance. Readings, a daily historical case study, and war gaming based on historical situations should be part of the curriculum.

Third, antique techniques must be abandoned. Attacking "on line" has been obsolete since the battle of Cold Harbor. Tactics and techniques must reflect maneuver warfare on the modern battlefield. Free-play exercises should be introduced early in the course. Lieutenants should be brought face-to-face with friction early in their education -- after all, it is the medium in which they will be expected to operate in combat. Only by encountering an active enemy who is trying to confuse, surprise and defeat them in an environment of uncertainty and rapid change can they begin to understand the nature of the business to which they have committed themselves.

The subjects of much of the current curricula at AWS and Command & Staff, such as writing skills, knowledge of nomenclature, staff procedures and basic techniques, should be entry requirements. Admission to both schools should require passing an examination in these subjects.

The time freed by elimination of these subjects from the courses of study should be devoted, first, to military history. The purpose of AWS and Command and Staff is educating officers, not producing academic historians. The purpose of studying history should be neither to memorize names, dates, and circumstances of battles, nor to learn formulas based on "what successful commanders always do" or some checklist of "principles of war." Rather it should be to learn how successful commanders think -- to study their thought processes.

Therefore, the teaching of history and the teaching of tactics and operations should be integrated. Most if not all historical study should be tactical and operational case studies. The instructor's job should be to take students through each case asking such questions as "What were this commander's options here? Did he perceive all of them? If not, why not? Why did he select the one he did? Was his decision quick enough to be useful? What might have been the consequences of alternative decisions?" While histories that focus on the commander's thought process are not common, they do exist: Rommel's Infantry Attacks is a good example. The faculties of the schools should be responsible for researching and writing others.

War gaming should play a much larger role in the courses of instruction. The purpose of gaming should not be to see who wins or loses, nor to attempt to "prove" certain specific approaches. There should be no "yellows," no school solutions. Rather, it should be to teach students to make quick decisions through a coherent, logical thought process, while under pressure. General F. W. von Mellenthin, a 1937 graduate of the German War College, has told of the frequency and importance of war gaming at that school. He stressed that there were no "right answers." A student was never told his decision was wrong. He was criticized for only two things: failure to make a timely decision, and inability to give a logical, coherent explanation for his decision. But if he made either of these errors, he was criticized severely.[3]

The games must of course permit maneuver warfare. Computerized games where the computer attempts to decide "who won" are worse than useless: the computer can only reward "kills,"

44

which means the game compels firepower/attrition warfare.
Computers must be restricted to doing calculations and providing
probability tables. Manual games are fully adequate, and a number
of commercially available games can be useful.

The faculties of both schools must also be improved. Quality
of education depends heavily on quality of faculty. Faculty
members must themselves be educated in the art of war. They must
also have the ability to critique someone else's thought process
-- a somewhat rare gift. To obtain such a faculty, the schools'
directors must have the authority to get whomever they want as
faculty, regardless of the person's career pattern and the desires
of the personnel shop at Headquarters Marine Corps. The faculty
so chosen must in turn be rewarded well. A three-year tour as a
faculty member, if satisfactorily completed, should bring either
early promotion or a highly sought follow-on assignment or both.

These reforms could make the schools at Quantico again what
they were in the inter-war years: dynamic, innovative centers of
education, where students are challenged to think critically.

Until then, what can you do? First, you can read. An
annotated bibliography of maneuver warfare readings is included in
this book. Second, you can war game, either alone or with fellow
officers. If you are a commander, you can make war games part of
your unit's duty-time activities. Third, you can organize
seminars in your unit or informally among officers who share your
interest in the art of war. You can use the seminars to discuss a
book you all have read, to hear a presentation about a battle or a
campaign, or to discuss a current tactical or operational
problem.

These three steps might not sound like much, but together they
can make a big difference in an officer's understanding of
maneuver warfare. Even after the schools are improved, all three
will continue to be necessary. Education is a continuing process.
It cannot be restricted to the relatively small amount of time
officers spend in schools. There is far more to be learned than
the schools can hope to teach. You will have to learn most of it
through your own independent efforts. Reading, war gaming and
seminars are three important components of any self-education
program.

Education is one part of preparing yourself to do maneuver
warfare successfully in combat. Training is another. What is the
difference between them?

Education is understanding the nature of war and learning how
to think logically and creatively about it and in it. Training is
the application of education. It is learning how to do maneuver
warfare in the "real world," the world of friction. If you want
to think of education as the classroom, training is the lab. It
is the place where you put your education to work on concrete
problems. Of course, training and education are not wholly
separate. Good training broadens your education. As you learn
how to do maneuver warfare through training, you also come to
understand it better.

If we look at training from the perspective of maneuver
warfare, we can identify four different aspects to it:

1. Basic techniques. These are things like firing a weapon, reading maps, physical conditioning, and so on. They are the same in maneuver warfare and in firepower/attrition warfare.
2. Advanced techniques. Advanced techniques include things such as unit skills, conducting a specific type of attack (e.g., a penetration), employing combined arms, and so on. In some cases, these are different in maneuver warfare from what they are in firepower/attrition warfare. For example:

- The attack by infiltration is often used in maneuver warfare, and it needs to be an important part of field training.
- The assault is conducted differently in maneuver warfare. Today, Marines use a two-element assault force. One element pins the enemy down while the other gets into his position and destroys him in close combat. In maneuver warfare, as noted earlier, the most common assault technique uses a three-element force: a large suppression element, a small penetrating element, and a large exploitation element. The suppression element makes the enemy keep his head down at the point of the assault. The penetrating element makes a small breach in the enemy's position. The exploitation element goes through the breach, fans out in the enemy's rear, and collapses his position from the rear. Some of the exploitation element immediately drives deeper into the enemy's rear, looking for surfaces and gaps, so the assault can immediately turn into an advance.

3. Building initiative and imagination among junior leaders. Initiative and imagination in junior leaders, including fire team and squad leaders, is very important in maneuver warfare. Training must seek to develop it. How can it do this?

One of the most important ways is by giving junior leaders opportunities to operate in a free-play, aggressed situation on the basis of mission orders. Free-play exercises are critical to developing initiative, imagination and new tactics. They present junior leaders with unpredictable, rapidly changing situations just like combat. This automatically brings initiative and imagination to the fore.

In addition, it is important these exercises allow junior leaders to make mistakes. "Zero defects" is a sure prescription for wooden, formal set-piece exercises that stifle initiative. Leaders who try new approaches should be praised for doing so, even when they don't work.

A good example of a way to train junior leaders to show initiative and imagination is provided by the Israelis. An Israeli battalion commander will take a company to the field and say, "You will be attacked in one hour by an enemy tank company. The tank company will not have infantry or artillery support. Prepare an appropriate defense." Forty-five minutes into the hour he will say, "The enemy tank company will have infantry, artillery and air support. Modify your defense appropriately." Then, with just five minutes left before the attack is due, he will say, "We have just learned that the attack will come from precisely the opposite direction from which we expected it. Again, modify your

defense appropriately." Then the battalion commander will hold a
critique, looking at how the company adapted to rapidly changing
circumstances.

4. Teaching leaders at all levels to live with friction.
Friction is the inherent condition of war. It is caused by the
enemy, by terrain and weather, and by the foul-ups that occur in
your own force. The only way to learn how to deal with it is to
train with it. Again, this means conducting aggressed, free-play
exercises. And it means taking the whole unit to the field. CPXs
have great value, but whenever troops are not involved, the level
of friction is unrealistically low. Units must get plenty of time
in the field as units if they are to learn how to accomplish their
missions despite friction.

Commanders can help inject friction into field exercises.
They can and should spring surprises on the participants. A good
example was provided in a recent maneuver warfare exercise by the
2nd Marine Division. The commander of the 2nd Division, Major
General A. M. Gray, Jr., had secretly arranged for a unit of the
82nd Airborne to make a parachute landing in the rear of one of
his own battalions and attack it. The result was good training.
A tank company that happened to be on the spot saw the situation,
acted on its own authority and attacked the paratroopers,
defeating them before they had even collected their chutes. By
presenting his battalion with an unexpected threat, General Gray
increased the level of friction and taught the importance of
mission orders and initiative to cope with and reduce that
friction.

How well do Marines train today? On the whole, not very well.
Units get too little time in the field as units. Recent inquiries
at Camp Pendleton found the average infantry battalion spent only
about 30 days a year in the field as a battalion. The tank
battalion had not gone to the field as a battalion once in the
previous twelve months. Free-play exercises are rare, except in
the 2nd Marine Division. Much training time is devoted to
preparing for elaborate, staged-managed ballets such as MCCRES,
CAX, and Solid Shield. Ammunition, fuel and time for training are
all inadequate.

Just as the schools at Quantico need reform, so does Marine
Corps training. Until that happens, what can you do?
You can set up local free-play exercises on the battalion and
company level. A free-play exercise devised and carried out
several years ago by the 1st Tank Battalion shows what can be done
locally. The whole battalion went to the field and conducted a
two-phase exercise. The first three days were company against
company. The rule was, "Any other company you encounter is
hostile," and the battalion commander gave orders that insured
companies would cross paths at unexpected times. After each
encounter, there was an immediate critique. The second three-day
phase saw augmentation of the tanks with two infantry companies in
Amtracks, some helicopters, FACs and FOs. The tank battalion also
introduced a recon platoon which it had created from its own
assets and mounted in jeeps. From these resources, an aggressor
force of a tank company, an infantry company (mounted), some TOWs
and some helicopters was formed. The tank battalion assigned the

aggressors a broad mission: prevent the friendly forces from passing through a certain area. They could defend, delay, launch a pre-emptive attack--whatever they wanted to do. Tank battalion headquarters made sure it did not know what the aggressor's plans were. Both forces had to rely on their own reconnaissance for information about the other.

The result was a series of surprises and counter-surprises -- just as in combat. Junior-level initiative was given a chance to flourish and it did, aided by the widespread use of mission orders. One participant said, "It was mass confusion, just like real war. We quickly learned not to be alarmed by disorder, but to use our commander's intent as a reference point and make our own decisions. We didn't shut down when things got confused, we just did what we thought we should to support the intent. And it worked."

Endex brought an immediate critique. There and afterwards, almost all the participants expressed great enthusiasm for the free-play approach, despite some inevitable troop training problems such as units getting bypassed and not having a chance to practice techniques. "Interesting" and "challenging" were the two words used most often to describe the exercise.

This exercise was carried out entirely at the initiative of the battalion. Other battalions can do the same. On a smaller scale, so can companies.

At least once a month, and if possible, more often, the officers should turn the unit over to the NCOs for the day and leave the area. This builds initiative and willingness to make decisions among NCOs. It also gives officers time to train themselves. A full day provides enough time to run a war game, take a staff ride, or conduct a seminar. The 2nd Marine Division has begun to do this on a division-wide basis, but it can also be done on the local level.

Learn how to critique. The value of exercises is very much a product of the quality of the critique, because it is in the critique that lessons can be drawn for all to see. Today, many critiques are poor quality. Often, they are not a critique at all, but just a narrative of who shot whom. At other times, the critique is stifled by an etiquette that demands no one be criticized and nothing negative be said. Too often, critiques can be summarized as "The comm was fouled up but we all did great."

There are a number of things you can do locally to improve the quality of critiques:

First, the commanding officer can set a ground rule that demands frankness in critiquing. A good way to encourage this is for the CO to give a trenchant self-critique of his own actions and encourage others to do the same. Beginning a critique with the most junior officers and ending up with the most senior can also help encourage frankness.

Second, a critique should be defined as something that looks beyond what happened to why it happened as it did. It may be helpful to look for instances where key decisions were made and ask the man who made them such questions as, "What options did you have here? What other options did you have that you failed to see? How quickly were you able to see, decide and act? If you

were too slow, why? Why did you do what you did? Was your
reasoning process sound, and if not, why not?"

Third, the unit commander can attempt to identify individuals
who are good critiquers and have them lead the critique. Not
everyone can do it well; it takes a certain natural ability.

Finally, the unit can hold a class on critiquing and from it
develop some critique SOPs. These can help exercise participants
look for key points during the exercise, points that can later
serve to frame the critique.

These actions are not substitutes for an overall reform of
Marine Corps training. But they are concrete ways you can improve
your own training. And just as individual self-education will be
important after the schools are reformed, so these actions will
help you train even after overall training is improved.

Education and training should work together to build common
approaches to problems, not common solutions. Both should prepare
you to know how to think in combat.

Conclusion

As stated in the Introduction, this book is not an academic dissertation, but a handbook. It has not attempted to cover everything, but rather to talk about those aspects of maneuver warfare platoon, company and battalion commanders need to understand. There are a number of very important issues that must be addressed at higher levels if the Marine Corps is to be able to do maneuver warfare in combat. They include:

- Promotions, assignments, selection for schools and graduation from schools must all be based on excellence, not fairness. Today, fairness is the driving consideration. Personnel management is largely concerned with giving everyone an equal chance to be promoted. Personnel are rotated at a dizzying rate to give as many people as possible a fair shot at getting a command. Standards in schools, standards of performance for those in command, standards in exercise critiques, etc. are all set so as to give the average officer who works hard a good chance of succeeding.

This approach is attractive in many ways, and it is consistent with contemporary society. It is the way most civilian institutions work, it is the basis of other government and many private promotion systems, and it has deep roots in American beliefs.

Unfortunately, it is not suitable for a military that wants to do maneuver warfare. In any military service, only a relatively few officers will have the ability to make and execute the kinds of decisions successful maneuver warfare requires. The basis and goal of the promotion and assignment system must be to put the few people capable of excellence in the key positions. The system must look at people as individuals, not sets of credentials and standardized fitness reports, in order to do this. Especially in regard to promotion in the higher ranks, it must not allow itself to be guided by clique or other bureaucratic politics. It must make every effort to find "the few who can do it," develop them, educate them, promote them, and give them key commands and staff positions.

- The Marine Corps must develop a professional NCO corps. Many Marines have seen a professional NCO corps in their training with the British Army and the Royal Marines. It has two basic

49

components: an NCO corps that lives, thinks and sees itself as separate from the troops and that is technically highly competent, and an officer corps that leaves NCO work to the NCOs.

Why is this necessary for maneuver warfare? If the officer's time is given largely or exclusively to the detailed, day-to-day running of the unit, he has little if any time to think about combat and the enemy. He becomes an expert in human relations, vehicle maintenance, marriage counselling, preparing for inspections -- in short, in all the things traditionally left to NCOs. When does he read military history? When does he do his war gaming, terrain walks, staff rides, and thinking about the art of war? Today, too often, he doesn't. He doesn't have time -- because he is running the unit himself. If the Marine Corps is to be able to do maneuver warfare, it must have an NCO corps that can run the unit on a routine basis, so its officers can become the tactical and operational experts they are supposed to be.

• Preparing to win in combat must be the highest priority in the allocation of time, dollars, and rewards, at every level and under all circumstances.

Today, it is not. Public statements and pep talks may tell you it is, but every Marine officer knows the real story. Training for combat, studying war, and all the other things that go to create tactical and operational excellence take a back seat to preparing for the grand opera productions known as CAX and MCCRESS, to the maintenance report, to inspections, even to such trivia as the Combined Federal Campaign and base beautification.

In 1982 the world witnessed a clash between a military that made preparing for war its highest priority and one that had many higher priorities, domestic politics chief among them. The two militaries were, respectively, the British and the Argentine. In terms of the priority the Marine Corps today gives to winning in combat, it is closer to the Argentines than to the British. That should deeply concern every Marine.

Changing priorities will require action beyond the Marine Corps. Certainly the Congress will have to support the effort if it is to succeed. But it will also take action from within the Corps, primarily at the highest levels but also, in the form of demands for change, from throughout the officer corps.

These and other similar issues should be subjects for thought for every Marine. Some of those now serving as lieutenants, captains, and majors will someday command MABs, MAFs, and the Marine Corps itself. The more carefully they consider these broad, long-term issues now, the better they will be able to direct policy then.

By that time, the Marine Corps will probably have gone far along the road toward maneuver warfare, not just in terms of doctrine, but also in relation to the changes needed to be able to do maneuver warfare in combat. Why such optimism? Because despite the inroads bureaucracy, promotion politics, and thinking by formula have made, Marines are still Marines. The dedication of a large majority of the non-commissioned and commissioned officer corps to military excellence is strong. Marines want to be the best. If that requires changing some established practices, then they support the changes. They are heirs to a great military tradition, a tradition that emphasizes innovative ideas as much as courage and fidelity. They have an esprit strong enough to challenge policies and practices that degrade combat effectiveness. And combat remains their focus of effort, the Schwerpunkt of everything they do.

The Marine Corps is challenged by maneuver warfare, but it is also given an opportunity -- the opportunity to be the lead service in a change of historic significance. That is the kind of opportunity Marines have always welcomed. There is every reason to believe they will welcome it today the same way they did in the 1920s and 1930s.

Notes

Introduction

1. Report to the Congressional Military Reform Caucus on the Grenada Operation, by William S. Lind, Military Reform Institute, April 5, 1984.

2. Quoted in The U.S. Marines and Amphibious War, Jeter A. Isley and Philip A. Crowl (Princeton University Press, Princeton, New Jersey, reprinted by the Marine Corps Association, Quantico, Virginia, 1979) p. 4.

Chapter 1

1. Colonel F. D. Sverdlov, <u>Tactical Maneuver</u>, translated in <u>Strategic Review</u> (Summer, 1983), p. 88.

2. Martin Van Creveld, <u>Command</u>, DoD Contract MDA-903-81-C-0480, pp. 256-260.

3. "Translation of Taped Conversation with General Hermann Balck, 13 April 1979," (Battelle Columbus Laboratories Tactical Technology Center, 505 King Avenue, Columbus, Ohio 43201) pp. 41-42.

Chapter 2

1. Captain B. H. Liddell Hart, "The 'Man-in-the-Dark' Theory of Infantry Tactics and the 'Expanding Torrent System of Attack," Journal of the R.U.S.I., (February 1921), p. 13.

2. Captain Timothy Lupfer, USA, The Dynamics of Doctrine: The Changes in German Tactical Doctrine During the First World War, (Ft. Leavenworth, KS: USA Command and General Staff College, 1981), pp. 15-16.

3. Small Unit Operations During the German Campaign in Russia, DA Pamphlet 20-269 (Washington: U. S. Army, 1953), pp. 58-62.

4. The idea of seeing the commander's intent and the mission as contracts was originated by Colonel John Boyd as was the concept of the Schwerpunkt as a harmonizing element or medium (p. 18).

5. Captain S. C. Hawkins, USA, "Blood and Iron on the Golan Heights," Marine Corps Gazette (January 1984), p. 65.

6. Examples taken from War as an Empirical Basis for the Arrangement of Map Exercises and Field Discussions, Curt Gallenkamp, General der Artillerie, Historical Division European Command, MS #C-079, Koenigstein, 17 March 1951, pp. 4-34. The author is most grateful to Colonel Michael D. Wyly, USMC for bringing this material to his attention.

7. Erwin Rommel, Attacks, (Athena Press, Inc., Vienna, VA: 1979), pp. 235-247.

8. Field Marshall Erich Von Manstein, Lost Victories, (Novato, CA: Presidio Press, 1982), p. 198.

9. Len Deighton, Blitzkrieg, (New York: Ballantine Books, 1979), p. 230.

Chapter 3

1. Much of the material in this chapter was provided by Captain R. S. Moore, USMC.

2. The newly written draft of OH 6-6, The Marine Rifle Squad, contains thirty pages of squad and fireteam formations.

3. See Captain R. S. Moore, USMC, "Two Teams for Rifle Squad," Marine Corps Gazette, September 1983.

4. OH 9-3 (Rev. A), Mechanized Combined Arms Task Forces, (Marine Corps Development and Education Command, 1980), pp. 31-37.

Chapter 4

1. Much of this chapter has been drawn from "Blitzkrieg from the Sea: Maneuver Warfare and Amphibious Operations," by Captain R. S. Moore, USMC, Naval War College Review, Jan-Feb, 1984.

2. VADM Daniel E. Barbey, USN (Ret.), MacArthur's Amphibious Navy, Seventh Amphibious Force Operations, 1943-1945, (Annapolis: U. S. Naval Institute, 1969), p. 44, 79-80.

3. U. S. Marine Corps, U. S. Marine Corps Operations in World War II, Central Pacific Drive, (Washington: Government Printing Office, 1966), pp. 53-71.

4. See OH 9-3 (Rev. A), Mechanized Combined Arms Task Forces, (Marine Corps Development and Education Command, 1980), pp. 31-33.

5. Major R. B. Neller, USMC, critique of "Maneuver Warfare and Marines," Amphibious Warfare Review, July 1983, dated 1 September 1983.

Chapter 5

1. Letter from BGen J. C. Breckinridge to Colonel J. C. Smith, dated 21 November 1934, J. C. Smith Papers, Marine Corps Historical Center.

2. "German Training and Tactics: An Interview with Colonel Pestke," <u>Marine Corps Gazette</u> (October, 1983), p. 61.

3. Author's discussion with Professor R. H. S. Stolfi.

Annotated Bibliography

The following annotated bibliography is provided to give students of maneuver warfare a basic reading list they can use to improve their understanding of the subject. A complete list of books and papers on maneuver warfare would not only be unmanageably long for a book such as this, it would be of little use to most officers, since many of the materials would be in foreign languages or generally unobtainable or both. This bibliography has been restricted to some basic works in English, all of which are fairly readily available. When possible, sources from which they can be obtained have been given.

Battelle Interviews with German Generals: Interview with General Hermann Balck, 12 January 1979; Interview with General Heinz Gaedke, 12 April 1979; Interview with General Hermann Balck, 13 April 1979 (published by Battelle Columbus Laboratories, Tactical Technology Center, 505 King Avenue, Columbus, Ohio 43201)

These interviews provide very valuable looks at specific questions, issues and techniques by two outstanding German officers. The Balck interviews are particularly useful; General Balck was probably the finest tank tactician of World War II, and his insights on the nature of tank warfare against the Russians cannot be overvalued. Two quotes illustrate the value of these papers. General Gaedke comments at one point about the Americans:

> If you will permit me to be a little critical, I have generally found that American tactical and operational command tends to follow a rigid pattern, a school situation. And, unfortunately, since WW II we Germans have imitated a good deal of this.
> When I attend the maneuvers of our 3rd Corps here in Koblenz, or other maneuvers, it seems to me that these exercises are too rigidly conducted. First, one always is shown a big, beautiful situation map that is marvelously and most completely prepared. Then you get meticulously briefed on all the circumstances. You're shown our forces over here

and over there is something labeled Objective Number One. What's that? That's what we want to take. So what is it? It turns out to be some hill, some piece of wooded terrain, or whatever. What happens when we take that? Why, then we go on to Objective Number Two.

There is no sign here of the ideas that we bludgeoned into all of us old General Staff officers: Possessing the terrain doesn't matter; what matters is to shatter the enemy and then the terrain will fall into your hands by itself. (p. 27-28)

General Balck notes, reflecting on commanders' tendency to rely on formal meetings and briefings for their information:

With von Mellenthin I had the following happen. He once said to me that I was moving around too much and breakfasting with the troops too often. I said "Come with me tomorrow and I'll show you something." We went forward, had a meeting with some front line officers, asked our questions about some relevant matters, and got some answers. So then I said to the officers "Let's go have lunch together." During lunch we asked the same questions and completely different facts came to light. I said to Mellenthin "You see why I go to eat with my people so often? Not because they cook so well, but because that's when I find out the truth."

These publications (and the others by Battelle listed in this bibliography) are hard to find; your best hope is to ask friends who have a good collection of military writings. But they are worth the effort to hunt them down. They are especially good training tools for use with NCOs and junior lieutenants, because they are readable and relevant to daily life in any military. They show how theory turns into practice --the hardest task maneuver warfare presents to Marines.

Asa A. Clark IV et. al. editors, The Defense Reform Debate: Issues and Analysis, (1984, The Johns Hopkins University Press, Baltimore, Maryland)

This is the first thorough treatment of the military reform movement, of which maneuver warfare is only one element. A collection of essays by some of the most prominent military reformers and their critics, it presents a balanced examination of the principles, promises, weaknesses and prospects of the reform movement. Military reform is likely to be one of the main defense issues of the 1980s, and while only the maneuver warfare aspect of the movement has had much influence on and in the Marine Corps thus far, all the arguments of military reform are likely to be heard in the future with increasing frequency. Marines who are interested in the future direction of the Corps would do well to become familiar with military reform, and this book is thus far the only one on the subject.

Karl von Clausewitz, <u>On War</u>, translated and edited by Michael
    Howard and Peter Paret, (Princeton; Princeton University
    Press, 1976; available from the Marine Corps Association
    bookstore)

This remains the classic work of modern military literature.
Much of it is difficult reading, but it is also essential,
especially the sections on friction in war. The reader should
make certain to get the Howard/Paret translation, which thus far
is only available in hardback. The paperback versions are a much
earlier translation which is almost unreadable.

Martin van Creveld, <u>Fighting Power</u> (Greenwood Press, Westport,
    Connecticut, 1982; available from the Marine Corps Association
    bookstore)

For the purposes of this study, Martin van Creveld, an Israeli
military historian, defines as fighting power everything other
than quantity and quality of equipment: officer selection,
officer training, NCO training, replacement systems, rewards,
doctrine, etc. In each category he then contrasts the American
Army in World War II with the Wehrmacht. What emerges is clear
pictures of two very different types of military institutions, one
consistent with firepower/attrition warfare, the other with
maneuver warfare. This book is "must reading" if you are to
understand how everything a military service is and does must
follow from maneuver doctrine if it is to be capable of maneuver
warfare in combat.

Trevor Dupuy, <u>A Genius for War</u> (Hero Books, Fairfax, Virginia,
    reprinted 1984; available from the Marine Corps Association
    bookstore)

Part of maneuver warfare is learning what it is; another part
is coming to understand how a military service should be
structured in order to do it successfully in combat.
<u>A Genius for War</u> is a history of an institution that promoted
military excellence with uncommon consistency for almost 150
years: the German General Staff.
This book is very valuable for its history of the early
General Staff, from its founding by the Prussian military
reformers after Prussia's disastrous defeat at Jena through the
period of the elder von Moltke. After that, it deteriorates
somewhat. It fails to deal adequately with the decline of the
General Staff under Kaiser Wilhelm II, and it wanders off into a
largely meaningless quantitative methodology in dealing with World
War II. But even with these flaws, it should be part of every
officer's personal library, as a means by which he can begin to
think about the "big picture" changes maneuver warfare is certain
to bring to the Marine Corps and to the American armed forces
generally.

Lieutenant Colonel John A. English, Canadian Armed Forces, A Perspective on Infantry (Praeger Publishers, New York, 1981; available from the Marine Corps Association bookstore)

This is probably the best book written about infantry tactics in at least the last ten years. It is "must reading" for every infantry officer. Using a historical and multinational perspective, it traces the basic themes in the evolution of infantry tactics (and, too often, their failure to evolve) in a way that makes them clear and understandable. It provides the reader with the "how to think" framework that is so essential in maneuver warfare. This book cannot be too highly recommended, not only to infantry officers, but to all those who work with and support the infantry.

General Heinz Guderian, Panzer Leader, (unabridged hardback from Zenger Publishing Company, Washington, D.C. 1979; abridged paperback from Ballantine Books, New York, 7th printing 1980; both available from the Marine Corps Association bookstore)

Guderian was the creator of Germany's Panzer forces, and this is his story of their birth, development, and employment during World War II. The discussion of the French campaign is especially useful, with its stress on the need for quick decisions, bold actions, an understanding of the operational art and, above all, speed. Guderian somewhat overstates the resistance he met in developing the Panzer divisions, but his views on their mis-employment by Hitler in Russian after 1941 are both valid and poignant in terms of Guderian's personal frustration.

Alistair Horne, To Lose a Battle; France, 1940 (Penguin Books, New York, reprinted 1982; available from the Marine Corps Association bookstore)

This is more a popular than a scholarly work, but it is valuable both for its discussion of Panzer tactics and for its depiction of the French high command during the critical days of 1940. It provides a stark illustration of the price that can be paid for putting bureaucratic concerns above the demands of the military art. The serious student of the French Army in the inter-war period will soon find this book superceded by a forthcoming volume by Lieutenant Colonel Robert Doughty of the West Point history department.

Jeter A. Isely and Philip A. Crowl, The U.S. Marines and Amphibious War (1951, Princeton University Press, reprinted 1979 by the Marine Corps Association; available from the Marine Corps Association bookstore)

Although this book has some useful discussion of aspects of maneuver warfare, especially in its comparison of U.S. Army and Marine Corps tactics, its real value is its focus on institutional history: how the Marine Corps developed amphibious doctrine during the inter-war period. The contrast between the openness of the Corps, and especially of Quantico, to experimentation and innovation in the 1920s and 1930s and the resistance to innovations, including maneuver warfare, today should concern every Marine officer. Isely and Crowl give a thorough and highly relevant description of how the Marine Corps did innovate as an institution at one time, and thus point the way to what Marines may be able to do in the future.

B. H. Liddell Hart, Strategy (Signet Books, New York, 1974; available from the Marine Corps Association bookstore)

This book contains the heart of Liddell Hart's thinking, his strategy of the indirect approach. The basic principal he espouses applies to tactics and operations as well, which makes this volume valuable to officers of all ranks. It is interesting to compare Liddell Hart's theory, which focuses on place, with John Boyd's, where time is the critical element.

Captain Timothy T. Lupfer, USA, The Dynamics of Doctrine: The Changes in German Tactical Doctrine During the First World War (Combat Studies Institute, U. S. Army Command and General Staff College, Ft. Leavenworth, Kansas 66027. Copies may be obtained free of charge by writing to the Combat Studies Institute)

No officer can hope to understand maneuver warfare well without understanding the doctrinal revolution that occured in the German army between 1914 and 1918. Captain Lupfer's excellent monograph is the best single source on the subject. It traces the development of both the offensive and defensive tactics of 1917-1918, explaining not only the ideas behind them but the process by which the German army as an institution came to adopt them. The importance of this work can best be shown by reflecting on the problems the Marine Corps is having in adjusting its doctrine in peacetime, while the Germans did it in the midst of a fight for Germany's continued existence, and on the fact that the Blitzkrieg of World War II was created by combining tanks with the infantry tactics of 1918. Indeed, from a German perspective American tactics, infantry and armor, are only now catching up to where the Germans were by 1918. Put this study on your "must read" list.

Edward Luttwak and Dan Horowitz, The Israeli Army (Harper & Row, New York, 1975)

The Israeli Army has been the most maneuver-minded post-World War II armed service, although its performance in this respect has declined markedly since the Yom Kippur War. Edward Luttwak's book is a valuable institutional history of this army, focused not on battles and campaigns but on the development of the army as an organization. Unfortunately, the best discussions are scattered throughout the text and must be searched out.

Field Marshal Erich von Manstein, <u>Lost Victories</u> (1955, reprinted
1982 by Presidio Press, Novato, California; available from the
Marine Corps Association bookstore)

Field Marshal von Manstein was probably the best operational
and strategic thinker in the <u>Wehrmacht,</u> and this book, his
memoirs, is an important tool for understanding those arts. The
section where he leads the reader through his thought process as
he developed the plan for the invasion of France in 1940 is
especially valuable. His Kharkov counteroffensive remains one of
the most notable examples of defensive maneuver warfare. In his
training manual for the 5th Mechanized Division, General Kirk
recommends that you read this book once a year for thirty years.
It's not bad advice.

Grady McWhiney and Perry D. Jamieson, <u>Attack and Die: Civil War
Military Tactics and the Southern Heritage</u> (1982, The
University of Alabama Press, University, Alabama; available
from the Marine Corps Association bookstore)

This book is controversial because of its thesis that
Confederate tactics were fixated on the offensive by the Celtic
cultural heritage of a large number of southerners. Whether that
thesis is right or not, the book is of great value to students of
maneuver warfare for its demonstration of the effect of the rifled
musket on tactics. The rifled musket, not the machine gun,
quick-firing artillery, or breech loading spelled the end to the
Napoleonic combination of the tactical offensive with the
operational offensive. But it took many years for armies to learn
the lesson, years of terrible losses as men were forced to assault
frontally, on line, into entrenchments manned by riflemen. The
infantry assault did not again become viable until the Germans
introduced infiltration tactics during World War I.
This book should be on every officer's reading list, but it is
especially valuable to lieutenants. The Basic School still
teaches the on-line attack. This will give recent graduates a
clear picture of what is likely to happen to them and their
platoon if they try it in combat. It may also lead them, and
perhaps their superiors as well, to wonder why TBS persists in
teaching an assault technique rendered invalid 120 years ago.

<u>Armored Warfare in World War II: Conference Featuring F. W. von
Mellenthin, Generalmajor a.D., German Army, May 10, 1979</u>
(published by Battelle Columbus Laboratories, Tactical
Technology Center, 505 King Avenue, Columbus, Ohio 43201)

About 70 pages of this paper consist of a discussion with
General von Mellenthin about armored warfare. The remainder is a
prepared text in which the general related a number of his
experiences on the Eastern Front. The discussion is valuable
because it addresses a number of specific questions such as night
combat, resupply, communications and reconnaisance. However, the
value is greatly enhanced if the reader is well familiar with the
basics of maneuver warfare beforehand; this should not be the
first thing on your reading list.

Major General F. W. von Mellenthin, Panzer Battles (Ballantine
     Books, New York, 1976; available from the Marine Corps
     Association bookstore)

     This is an excellent account of German armored warfare in
World War II. It is a good companion to Field Marshal von
Manstein's Lost Victories, since von Mellenthin focuses more on
the tactical level, von Manstein more on the operational. Von
Mellenthin writes to give present-day soldiers and Marines a feel
for the Soviets as opponents, not just to write history. While
the scope of the fighting he describes is almost overwhelming to
Marines -- in one battle in 1941 the Germans took prisoner four
times the number of men in today's Marine Corps -- the lessons are
still valuable.

General George S. Patton, War As I Knew It (Bantam Books, New
     York, third printing 1981; available from the Marine Corps
     Association bookstore)

     Patton was the outstanding American practioner of maneuver
warfare on the tactical level during World War II, and this is his
own story of his campaigns. Although something of an exercise in
self-glorification, this book outlines the ideas which guided
Patton's actions. The bulk of the book is devoted to the Third
Army.

Proceedings of Seminar on Air Antitank Warfare, May 25-26, 1978
     (published by Battelle Columbus Laboratories, Tactical
     Technology Center, 505 King Avenue, Columbus, Ohio 43201)

     The focus of this paper is air antitank warfare, and it
includes a discussion with Colonel Hans Ulrich Rudel, the
Luftwaffe's famous tank-busting Stuka pilot. But the first half
of the paper is much broader, and is of direct interest to
students of maneuver warfare. It includes the transcription of a
talk by Colonel John Boyd in which he talks about the evolution of
his "OODA Loop" theory of conflict and about Blitzkrieg. Of equal
interest is the second section, also a discussion of Blitzkrieg.
To get full value from this study, the reader needs a good basic
understanding of maneuver warfare, so this should not be the first
thing you read.

Field Marshall Erwin Rommel, Attacks (1937, republished 1979 by
     Athena Press, Vienna, Virginia; available from the Marine
     Corps Association bookstore)

     This is one of the rare histories where the author attempts to
lead the reader through his thought process as he made decisions
in combat, and as such it is especially valuable to the student of
maneuver warfare. First published in 1937, it is Rommel's account
of his experiences as a small-unit infantry commander in the First
World War, experiences which won him the Pour le Merite. Most
valuable from the standpoint of maneuver warfare is the account of
the battle of Caporetto, during which Rommel, leading a force of

battalion size, captured over 10,000 prisoners. Since it was written for German officers, the book presumes a knowledge of the change in German infantry tactics during World War I from the linearity of 1914 to the infiltration tactics of 1918. The modern American reader will get much more out of the book if he first reads a good study of that change such as Captain Timothy Lupfer's The Dynamics of Doctrine.

Captain Adolf von Schell, Battle Leadership, (1933, reprinted 1982
     by the Marine Corps Association; available from the Marine
     Corps Association bookstore)

     Captain von Schell was a company commander in the German Army on the eastern front during World War I. Unlike the western front where trench warfare predominated, the eastern front was fluid, and mobile warfare was the rule. His experiences, related in this volume, are of great value to junior infantry officers because they illustrate what maneuver warfare means on the small unit level. This short quote about peacetime training gives the flavor of the book:

     In our peace-time map problems, war games and field exercises,
     we have simple solutions. There is no uncertainty, nothing
     goes wrong, units are always complete . . . In war it is quite
     otherwise. There is no situation that our imagination can
     conjure up which even remotely approaches reality. In peace
     we have only grammar school tactics. But let us never forget
     that war is far more advanced than a high school. Therefore,
     if you would train for the realities of war, take your men
     into unknown terrain, at night, without maps and give them
     difficult situations. In doing so use all the imagination you
     have. Let the commanders themselves make their decisions.
     Teach your men that war brings such surprises and that often
     they will find themselves in apparently impossible situations
     . . . Every soldier should know that war is kaleidoscopic,
     replete with constantly changing, unexpected, confusing
     situations. Its problems cannot be solved by mathematical
     formulae or set rules. (p. 63)

     This is a short book - just 95 pages -- and it can be read easily in an evening. It is as relevant today as it was when it was first published more than 50 years ago. Indeed, it may be the best single book on maneuver warfare for the platoon and company commander, despite all that has been written since.

U. S. Army Historical Publications (obtainable from Department of
     the Army, Military History (ATTN: DAMH-ZF), Pulaski Building,
     20 Massachusetts Avenue, NW, Washington, D.C.   20314

     The Army has published and made available a number of specialized historical publications, concentrating on German practices during World War II. These are quite useful to the student who wants to explore a particular aspect of maneuver warfare in greater depth. Publications include German Defense Tactics Against Russian Breakthroughs, German Antiguerrilla Operations in the Balkans, and Small Unit Actions During the German Campaign in Russia.

Captain G. C. Wynne, If Germany Attacks: the Battle in Depth in the West (1940, reprinted in 1976 by Greenwood Press, Westport, Connecticut; available from the Marine Corps Association bookstore)

This book describes in detail the evolution of German defensive tactics during World War I from the rigid, linear trench fighting of 1915 through the elastic, "let them walk right in" tactics of 1917-1918. It is a good follow-up to Captain Timothy Lupfer's monograph The Dynamics of Doctrine for those who want to explore the history of defensive maneuver warfare. Although the defenses it describes were developed for and by infantry, the same concepts provided the basis for German armor defensive tactics in World War II.

Tang Zi'Chang, trans., Principles of Conflict: Recompilation and New English Translation with Annotation on Sun Zi's Art of War, (1969, T. C. Press, San Rafael, California)

Sun Zi is better known as Sun Tzu, but however you spell it his Art of War is a maneuver warfare classic. This is the best English translation; Tang Zi'Chang was a general in the army of the Republic of China, and he re-ordered Sun Tzu's aphorisms so as to make the ideas more comprehensible to fellow soldiers. If you cannot find this particular translation, get another, but in any case read the book -- and re-read it.

Appendix:
Fundamentals of Tactics

Colonel Michael D. Wyly, USMC

Foreword

William S. Lind

Many Marines are confused about the Marine Corps' position on maneuver warfare. Is maneuver warfare now doctrine? Has it spread beyond the 2nd Marine Division? Is it taught in the schools? Is it doctrine?

The following material is a partial answer to these questions. It is a series of lectures delivered to the Amphibious Warfare School by the then-head of the Tactics Department, Colonel Michael D. Wyly, USMC, in the 1981-82 school year. The lectures on surfaces and gaps, mission tactics, and the main effort were given to the entire school; those on the objective and the reserve to Colonel Wyly's den. They have been reproduced here essentially as given, along with the problems that accompanied them.

At the time these lectures were given, what they present -- maneuver warfare, although the term is not used in them -- could have been considered doctrine. It was taught as tactics at AWS. But it is not what is taught there today. These lectures are no longer delivered. Under different leadership, AWS, along with Command and Staff, have fallen back to a different set of "fundamentals," to memorizing terms, being very concerned with formats, and testing a student's knowledge of tactics with multiple choice and fill-in-the-blank tests. In short, they have fallen back to teaching what to do and what to think, not how to think.

Officer education that is focused on teaching what to do and what to think implies a doctrine of firepower/attrition warfare, since that is the only kind of warfare officers so educated will be able to undertake. So is firepower/ attrition warfare now doctrine?

The answer is that doctrine, like many other things in today's Marine Corps, is in a state of flux. Maneuver warfare adherents are gaining ground, but many senior officers continue to prefer "business as usual." Whether a given school or unit practices maneuver warfare or continues the old-style, rigid, stylized approach to combat that characterizes attrition warfare is largely a product of who is in command. As commanders change, so, in effect, does doctrine.

70

But on the whole, the direction of movement is toward maneuver warfare. Colonel Wyly's excellent lectures show how far things have come. A few years ago the subjects of his lectures were, in large part, unknown except to military historians. Now, even if they are no longer given at Quantico, they have been heard by one entire AWS class.

The day will come when the schools at Quantico will once and for all agree that Colonel Wyly has correctly defined the fundamentals of tactics. Maneuver warfare will be doctrine, sooner or later. Until then, maneuver warfare will probably progress two steps forward, then one backward. For Marines caught up in the ebb and flow, this can be frustrating and is almost certainly confusing. For students who have had to endure AWS since Colonel Wyly's departure and the re-emphasis on forms and terms, it means an important opportunity lost.

But reading these lectures offers at least partial recompense. They are easy to read, intellectually sound, and offer not only good material but a useful model for other instruction. The analysis that follows each problem is especially useful, because it shows how to critique a solution without falling into the "school yellow" trap on the one hand or the fog of "everything is OK" on the other.

Someday, both the material in this appendix and the style of teaching it represents will be routine. Until then, it adds substantially to this book through its substance and by showing what one officer can accomplish through his own initiative. On both counts, it is of great use to any Marine interested in maneuver warfare and in the future of the Corps.

Introduction

What follows is a basic course in tactics. It is a compilation of lectures and problem exercises, esentially as I presented them at the Marine Corps Amphibious Warfare School in the fall of 1981. I gave them in the first semester as a precursor to more complex work that was to come. This course is designed for the student who has no background in tactics, academic or practical, but it will also be helpful to the experienced student who is interested in learning modern tactics as opposed to the more rigid, slower moving form of warfare that was practiced and taught in the past.

I call this course "Fundamentals of Tactics." I chose the name because it endeavors to ferret out and present in their simplest form those things that are most basic to the successful conduct of battle.

When I initially designed the course I was warned that it might not be comprehensible to those of my students who had little or no previous experience in tactics. My course thrusts the beginning student into the position of a battalion or company commander and requires him to make tactical decisions. Skeptics advised that students should first be subjected to the traditional classes in which they learn the language of tactics. They should be taught definitions such as what a line of departure is and how an axis of advance differs from a direction of attack. They must know that the line of departure is crossed at H-hour. They had to understand boundaries and zones of action. Until they knew these things, they could not solve the problems. And certainly, said my critics, the students must know the formats into which the operation orders must be put before they think about what kind of orders they are going to issue. In brief, I was told that the student should first learn the fundamentals.

However, it seemed to me that the fundamentals of tactics were neither definitions nor control measures nor formats. It seemed to me that what was <u>fundamental</u> to tactics was that which dealt with defeating the enemy. The answer to the question of what will work to undo the opposing force is what we must be searching for in tactics. That must be what the student comes to grips with when he studies tactics. All else is peripheral.

In retrospect, I became critical of much of the tactical training I had received as a student. The single most important criticism that leapt at me was that in teaching me tactics my instructors had always placed me in boxes. First, I was taught the formats into which my thinking would have to fit -- a mental box. Then when I was finally thrust into a problem-solving situation, before I was turned loose to make tactical decisions I was placed in a second box. They called it a zone of action. It was defined by a line of departure on my end, a boundary on at least one if not both sides, and a thing called an objective on the far end: a terrain-oriented linear box. Having been put in these boxes, I must say I found it difficult to maneuver freely, to think creatively, and to do the things that would be most destructive to the enemy. It was for this reason that I decided to teach tactics in a somewhat different mode than had been followed before.

Terminology, control measures and formats must all be learned. We must speak a common language if we are to continue to be the cohesive Corps that we are. The Basic School and subsequent schools must continue to stress a common language that is understood by all Marines so that we fight as a single team. Teamwork has long been our trademark. It is indispensable.

But first the student must learn to think creatively, to innovate, and to do the things that will most quickly seek out the enemy's weak spots and undo him. Learning to think in that fashion is fundamental. That is what this course is about: the fundamentals. Once these fundamentals are learned, that is, once the student has begun to think clearly about how best to undo his adversary, once he has been rewarded in the classroom or the field for creative thought, the careful weighing of alternatives and risks followed by boldness in decision-making, he will then be ready to study definitions, control measures and formats. He will grasp their meaning more rapidly, for he will have a context in which to place them. They will be more than mere words and symbols.

When we teach tactics in the opposite order, that is, the mechanics ahead of the thinking, too often we produce, instead of soldiers, structured mechanics who find it difficult to think without rules. The art of war has no traffic with rules. Yet I have often seen students reject their best tactical ideas because they could not fit them into the format.

My problem exercises are without boundaries and lines of departure. The time of attack is the student's call. He bases it on the enemy, what the enemy is doing now, not two hours ago when the order was given. The student can indicate what he would do off the edges of the map. Does he know how the terrain is formed there? No. But will you always know in combat? Not always. It is up to the student to think about what possible terrain forms and, more importantly, enemy activities might hinder or help him in the execution of his operation.

Much thought and discussion and no little amount of pain and anguish have gone into trying to answer the question, "What are the fundamentals?" I submit that the fundamentals are the concepts that follow.

Lecture I:
Surfaces and Gaps

The concept of surfaces and gaps is one of several concepts that bear on tactics. It is of the same level of importance as mission tactics and the main effort, which will be the subjects of the two tactics lessons following this one. All of the concepts should be constantly at work during the execution of battle.

It is unimportant whether you refer to this concept as surfaces and gaps or soft spot tactics or simply the idea of pitting your strength against the enemy's weakness. That is what it is all about, strength against weakness, call it what you will. The term surfaces and gaps is derived from a German term, Flaechen und Luekentaktik, which means simply, the tactics of surfaces and gaps, the surfaces being the enemy's strong points, which we avoid, the gaps being the weak points that we go through. We often hear of Flaechen und Luekentaktik being referred to as von Hutier tactics, von Hutier being the name of the commander of the 18th German Army on the western front, who had particular success using this form of warfare. Von Hutier did not invent the tactic. However his name is still attached.

Basil Liddell Hart, the British author, called it the expanding torrent system tactic. He drew an analogy between an attacking army and a torrent of water:

> If we watch a torrent bearing down on each successive bank of earth and dam in its path, we see that it first beats against the obstacle feeling it and testing it at all points. Eventually, it finds a small crack at some point. Through this crack pour the first driplets of water and rush straight on. The pent up water on each side is drawn towards the breach. It swirls through and around the flanks of the breach, wearing away the earth on each side and so widening the gap. Simultaneously the water behind pours straight through the breach between the side eddies which are wearing away the flanks. Directly it is passed through it expands to widen once more the onreach of the torrent. Thus as the water pours through in ever-increasing volume the onreach of the torrent swells to its original proportions, leaving in turn each crumbling obstacle behind it.

The idea of putting <u>Flaechen und Luekentaktik</u> into practice
was first implemented by the German Army in World War I. In 1918,
as they prepared for Ludendorff's Spring Offensive, the German
Army changed its offensive tactics. The Germans had found that
they were being overpowered by the material available to the
British and French. The Americans were coming and it was clear
that Germany was going to lose if she did not do something
differently. Because they did not have the option of matching the
allies' strength in material, the Germans decided that they would
have to outthink them. That is, they would have to have better
tactics.

Germany did not succeed in winning the war. It was too late
by this time. They were surrounded. The women and children were
starving at home. It was simply too late for them to win. Yet,
they made some tactical progress there at the last in the spring
of 1918. They inflicted terrible defeats on their enemies to the
point that the allied armies were seriously considering the
prospect of giving up.

At the tactical level, the Germans put their strength against
weakness. They sought the gaps. Small assault groups called
<u>Sturmgruppen</u> sought gaps in the enemy lines and attacked through
them, assaulting with light machine guns, rifles, grenades, and
flamethrowers, while heavy machine guns, direct and indirect fire
weapons, including trench mortars, were used to suppress the enemy
strong points.

But on the strategic level, the Spring 1918 Offensive failed.
Why? Because Ludendorff, on that level, put strength against
strength. Though he was seeking gaps, he was seeking gaps at the
enemy's strong points. He committed his reserves before the enemy
committed his, and his offensive bogged down.

<u>Flaechen und Luekentaktik</u> is an old term, dating from World
War I, when tactics, compared to today's, were quite linear. One
should not confuse the idea with linearity. It remains a useful
concept if thought of in non-linear modern terms. Gaps are weak
points. Surfaces are strong points. They are not necessarily
strong and weak points along a line, like a dotted line of
alternative dashes and spaces.

The idea of putting strength against weakness was, of course,
born way before 1918. Clausewitz writes about it in Chapters 9
and 10 of Book 7. In Chapter 9, regarding defensive positions, he
states:

> The attack cannot prevail against them. It has no means at
> its disposal to counteract their advantage. In practice, not
> all defensive positions are like this. If the attacker sees
> that he can get his way without assaulting them, it would be
> stupid of him to attempt it. It is a risky business to attack
> an able opponent in a good position.

Chapter 10 is entitled, "Attack on Entrenched Camps." Says
Clausewitz:

> Not only reason, but hundreds and thousands of examples show
> that a well prepared, well manned and a well defended

entrenchment must generally be considered as an impregnable
point and is indeed, regarded as such by the attacker. If we
proceed from this factor of the effectiveness of a single
trench, we cannot really doubt that the assault on an
entrenched camp is a very difficult and usually an impossible
task for the attacker. The offensive should only very rarely
resort to an attack on an entrenched camp. Such an attack is
advisable only if the defenses have been executed hurriedly,
left incomplete, and lack obstacles to access, or in general
if, as often happens, the camp is a mere sketch of what it
ought to be, a half completed ruin. Then an attack may be
advisable and an easy way to vanquish the enemy.

Employment of this concept of surfaces and gaps, then, gives
us many advantages over what could be called slower moving forms
of combat, where strength is thrown against strength. Attacking
through gaps, avoiding surfaces, gives us an advantage of economy
of force. If we are pitting strength against strength, assaulting
enemy strong points, we are consuming our manpower as well as
ammunition and supplies as we go along. If we go through the
gaps, we are practicing economy of force. We are reaching our
objective without using up our men. We are leaving the enemy
behind. Because we are moving faster, we have the advantage of
rapid exploitation.

Let us look first at the gaps and determine what we are
talking about. We may look for already existing gaps or we may
create gaps, but we prefer to find them already existing.
Creating gaps takes time. It consumes resources, usually in the
form of casualties. Therefore, exploiting ready-made weak spots
is more efficient.

It may help to start with a very simple example, perhaps
overly simple, but simple things can help us to understand.
Envision yourself with mission to get your force from Berlin in
the East to Paris in the West. The enemy defensive line lies in
between. If you can discover portions of the enemy line where the
defenses are stretched thin, undermanned, or poorly manned you
have discovered gaps - opportunities for your attack. This is old
fashioned and linear but it may aid in understanding here in the
beginning. We will come to more modern examples later on. If our
mission is simply to get to Paris, clearly we are going to get
there a lot faster if we go through the gaps. So, how do we find
them? There is a multitude of methods. We will discuss a few.

First, the reconnaissance screen. This is what we call the
reconnaissance pull technique as opposed to command push. Your
reconnaissance is always preceding the main body and its mission
out there is to find the gap. I am not talking about Force
Reconnaissance or Reconnaissance Battalion. This is not a mission
for specialized reconnaissance forces. Any company commander, any
battalion commander, should have a reconnaissance screen of some
sort in front of him, drawn from his own troops. What kind of
vehicles it uses, if any, and what it is armed with are going to
be dependent on the situation. It should be at least as mobile as
the main body, however. Preferably more so. If it is less mobile

than the main body, its function will necessarily be temporary and intermittent.

The reconnaissance screen might be a company deployed over a very broad front. But its mission is not to attack. Its mission is to find the gaps. When it finds them, it relays this information back, so that the main body can push on through the gap. Gaps are found by delegating authority down to the lowest level, so that small unit commanders can find gaps and immediately start exploiting them without delay. If we are always going to wait for directions from above, our force is going to be very slow moving, so this concept of surfaces and gaps depends on initiative at low levels.

The concept of surfaces and gaps demands leadership from the front as opposed to leadership from the rear. The commander must be where he can make swift decisions. He must be where the situation is developing. Obviously, leadership from the front had become a scarcity by World War I. J. F. C. Fuller, in his book, Generalship, wrote:

> In the World War, nothing was more dreadful to witness than a chain of men, starting with a battalion commander and ending with an army commander, sitting in telephone boxes, improvised or actual, talking, talking, talking, in place of leading, leading, leading.

The result was unresponsive leadership and slow reactions.

Now let us complicate the subject a little. We began looking simply at our route from Berlin to Paris. We had to get through a line that had gaps in it. This was linear and old fashioned. Certainly, combat is not going to be that simple. The gap, then, might be any undefended point or any weakly defended point. It may be any enemy vulnerability. It might be the enemy's flanks.

The term flank itself needs some elaboration. Think of it as a relative thing. John Boyd defines a flank as "that aspect towards which a force is not devoting its primary attention." In other words, in fluid warfare, what is one moment the enemy's flank might the next moment be the enemy's front. It depends on how he is directing his attention. A gap for the infantry could be an enemy missile site manned by troops who are not combat oriented. The missile site might be a surface if you are flying an airplane but a gap if you are a light infantryman who has gotten inside the enemy lines.

Let us say that we are unsuccessful in finding any gaps at all. We may have to create gaps and there are ways of doing this. First, let us look at what the Germans call Stosstruppentaktik. This is the sequence of suppression, assault and exploitation. In other words, we punch our way through. Usually, it is costly. This is why we prefer to find gaps. But do not forget the first word of the sequence: suppression. Suppress the enemy to make him get his head down, and the assault should follow immediately on the heels of the suppression. Use artillery and mortars to suppress. Usually they have a more valuable function in suppressing than they do for actually inflicting casualties. They may inflict lots of casualties, but the real value you derive is from the suppression effect.

Although suppression is certainly the most valuable effect of artillery and air, there are two other effects which should not be discounted. Those are disruption and attrition. Disruption quickens the enemy's undoing. Attrition is helpful to your cause, but its effect on the enemy is realized most slowly of the three.

The assault should follow suppressive fires in seconds, as soon as possible. While the enemy is suppressed, we punch a small assault force through. Assault forces in this method are generally characterized by relative smallness. Small units are manageable.

It is the reserve -- or exploitation force -- that is characterized by relative bigness. After we have successfully created the gap, we exploit by getting as many of our reserves through as quickly as we can. If we have friendly forces pinned down on the right and left, the best way to get pressure off them is to get in deep behind the enemy.

Another way of creating gaps is through supporting attacks. By attacking one point along the line we may divert the enemy from another point and by drawing him off, create a gap. Again, this is in linear terms for instructional purposes, for simplicity. But do not get a linear mind-set. Sometimes a less costly way of creating a gap is through deception, by causing the enemy to think that we will attack at one point, thereby enticing him to draw his forces off from another point. And we attack at that point where he has weakened himself.

But what do we do about surfaces, that is, the strong points? Sometimes they are best bypassed. Once the enemy has been bypassed, his strong point may be cut off from its support and in that way his strong point eventually withers away and becomes a weak point which we can attack later.

Fire suppression is a means of neutralizing the strong points so that we can bypass them safely. Remember that the essential element of effective fire suppression is always time. Hours and hours of bombardment may not give you the desired effect, if you then lift your fire and try to attack too late, hoping you have killed the enemy. Artillery's function in suppression is neutralizing the enemy to give you time to accomplish your mission. Smoke or poison gas can be used to this same effect, that is, preventing the enemy from seeing you, and preventing the enemy from reacting against you.

A holding or pinning attack may be a means of dealing with the surface. This is a limited objective attack not designed to annihilate the enemy in the particular strong point, but rather to neutralize or preoccupy him so that your operation can continue to bypass or attack at another point.

Another means of dealing with a strong point is the infiltration attack. This may be seen as surfaces and gaps at the micro level. That is, instead of throwing a rigid line of assault troops into the enemy, our assault force seeks gaps in the enemy strong point and infiltrates into it. Often, this is best accomplished at night.

There are certain problems presented by the concept of surfaces and gaps, especially to commanders who are used to slow moving forms of combat. One is that the commander will not always know where all his people are. In the Marine Corps we have become used to being accountable at all times, for knowing exactly where every man is. In this faster moving form of combat, to do so would be impossible. Your subordinates are out finding the gaps and exploiting them.

Another problem is that artillery and air may not be controlled as closely as is possible in slower moving forms of combat. The desired effect is that the faster pace of our operations will keep the enemy off balance so that he can inflict fewer casualties on us. There is always the danger that artillery and air may strike our forces. Of course, we do everything we can to prevent that. But in the final analysis, we come out better if we keep our tempo moving faster than the enemy's. After all, he is trying to direct his fire against us. We may have some casualties resulting from errors but our control measures help prevent this. The result of faster tempo on our side will be fewer casualties on our side and a quicker victory.

Another problem associated with the concept of surfaces and gaps is that as we penetrate deeply, often on narrow fronts, our flanks become exposed. There are, however, compensating factors, again related to speed. We are moving quickly. The enemy is always off balance. Remember the old adage, "there is security in speed." Other friendly penetrations, nearby, in deep thrusts can reduce enemy pressure more efficiently than slower, plodding "flankers" that characterize slower moving forms of combat. The Germans had a term called <u>Aufrollen</u>, which means, literally, "thrusting upon." If you are attacking in one direction, you may

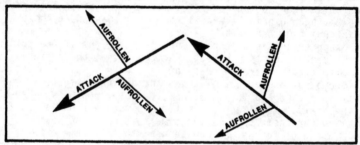

make minor attacks to the left and right of your main attack going out tangentially on narrow fronts and protecting your flanks in that way. Here speed is not sacrificed. If the main body slows down to the pace of flankers on the left and right, speed is sacrificed.

One of the problems that comes to mind in studying this concept focuses on the Soviet so-called "fire sack defense." Again, this relates to the need to modernize this concept and ensure it is non-linear. Note the diagram:

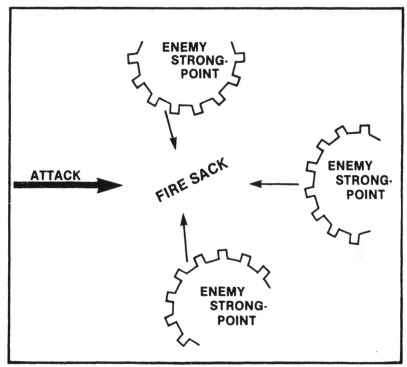

There are three Soviet strong points surrounding a fire sack. The desire is to draw the enemy into the fire sack so that he can be reduced from the surrounding strong points. If we look rigidly at the concept of surfaces and gaps, then we would see ourselves going through the gap, bypassing the strong point and ending up in the fire sack exactly where the enemy wants us.

The student must understand that the concept of the gap is a relative concept. The commander must evaluate each new situation. He must determine which are surfaces and which are gaps. There are no rules for this, but the fire sack, though it may appear as a gap, because there are no enemy, is actually a surface. It is a hard spot. It is a place where we are vulnerable. In this situation the gap may well be the strong point because if we can reduce one of the mutually supporting strong points, perhaps by an infiltration attack, we have then weakened the enemy and made him vulnerable. A Marine officer once commented to me in discussing this concept that he felt, were he commanding a unit seeking out enemy gaps, he would probably find himself right in the middle of a fire sack. So he may have. But I had to remind him of the interview with German General Hermann Balck. Balck states that warfare is an art. And like any art, there are only certain great artists. As Balck said, everyone cannot expect to be a Raphael. Clearly, this officer was not a Raphael. It is an art, distinguishing surfaces from gaps. That is why you should study history. It will help you see the distinctions.

Critics of these faster moving forms of combat characterized by initiative at the low level fear that they will lead to groups of men moving willy-nilly about the battlefield and that commanders will lose control. This need not be so. If the concept of surfaces and gaps is employed properly, it will not be so. That is why we have control measures. The boundary, the limit of advance, the phase line, can still be used. It must be remembered that these control measures should serve their function, but not be rigid lines that cannot be changed or ignored when the situation changes. They should be kept to a minimum and must always be flexible. The tactics must never follow the control measures. On the contrary, the control measures must follow the tactics. And the tactics must always be based on the enemy. Other concepts that will be discussed in the chapters ahead, especially that of the main effort, give us means of keeping control over our troops and preventing a situation where they can be said to be moving willy-nilly about the battlefield.

Exercise Number 1

SURFACES AND GAPS

PART I

1. You are Commanding Officer, Company B, 1st Bn, 5th Marine Regiment. It is 1200 on 21 September. You have a section of TOW, Wire-guided Missiles (8 TOW's), and a platoon of Amphibious Assault Vehicles (AAV's) (enough to lift everyone) under your command. 81mm mortars and 155mm artillery are in direct support. You cannot depend on air superiority. The situation in the air reverses almost hourly and is unpredictable. Your chain of command is depicted below.

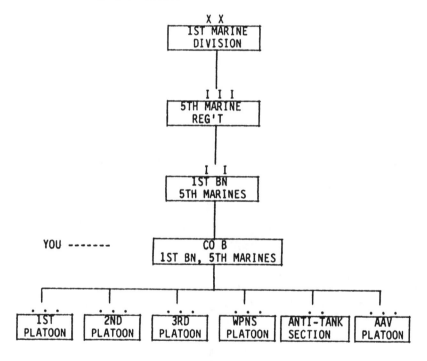

PART II

1. You know that your regiment (5th Marines) has this mission: Seize the Roadstown logistic base in order to force the enemy main force to fight on terrain of our choosing, disrupt his communications, and deny him the use of Roadstown rail heads.

2. You know that your battalion (1st Bn, 5th Marines) has this mission:
Advance as rapidly as possible towards Roadstown guiding on Route #8. Attack enemy forces encountered en route in order to ensure that they do not slow the movement of the regiment's motorized-mechanized column to Roadstown. Do not, however, allow the presence of enemy forces to draw you more than about 5000 meters away from Route #8 on either side. Revert to regimental reserve upon reaching Roadstown city limit.

3. You know that Company A has been designated the "main effort" of the battalion; that the battalion is supposed to get to Roadstown ahead of enemy reinforcements and that Company A's mission was stated in exactly the same words as the battalion's.

4. Your (Company B's) mission is as follows:

Advance to Roadstown as rapidly as possible attacking enemy units en route in order to hasten progress of Company A. Be prepared to assume the mission of Company A at any time.

5. As your platoons arrive at the position shown on your map, you receive this message:

Company A's progress is halted near Karl's Junction in heavy contact with enemy tanks and infantry. No change in orders.

6. Company A's position is at point K (see map). Battalion mortars are at point L. Note the arc indicating their range.

7. The entire map is in the artillery fan.

8. Company C and Tank Company (-) remain in battalion reserve. The battalion commander has signalled no intention to commit his reserve. One platoon of tanks is with Company A.

9. You have a reconnaissance screen, drawn from your own company, consisting of three mobile patrols moving ahead of you, patrols that you assigned from members of your company. They are presently at points P, Q and R. They moved to these points by the routes shown.

You have received reports from each, as follows:

Patrol at Point P: "We just clashed with a squad-sized enemy patrol. They withdrew to the North. I have two wounded, on the way to your position."

Patrol at Point Q: "No enemy sighted enroute to this position. We're about to continue moving north. We have a man up the power stanchion. A group of enemy officers and NCO's at the farm houses (Point S) is surveying the area, apparently trying to get organized. No troops in force there. Five trucks are unloading supplies along the road (Point T). Dust clouds indicate there may be enemy tanks deploying in the field (Point U)."

Patrol at Point R: "We're surrounded. I've got two badly wounded, bleeding heavily. I'll need help to get them out. Everytime we move we draw automatic fire and mortars."

PART III

WHAT DO YOU DO NOW?

1. Other than relaying the information from your patrols at P, Q and R, what communications do you send to higher headquarters, if any?

2. If you are going to move a unit or units, give them a point on the ground to aim for by drawing a circle around the point of their destination in the manner that you would designate a terrain objective.

3. If you plan for any of your units to move you must depict their movement graphically by means of a green arrow extending from the unit's location on the map and terminating at the circle that you draw for requirement #2. If you draw no arrows connected to a unit, we assume that you leave that unit in place (in this exercise, don't worry about moving your mobile reconnaissance patrols, P, Q and R).

4. Describe in the space below what is the main effort and main purpose of your action that you have shown graphically.

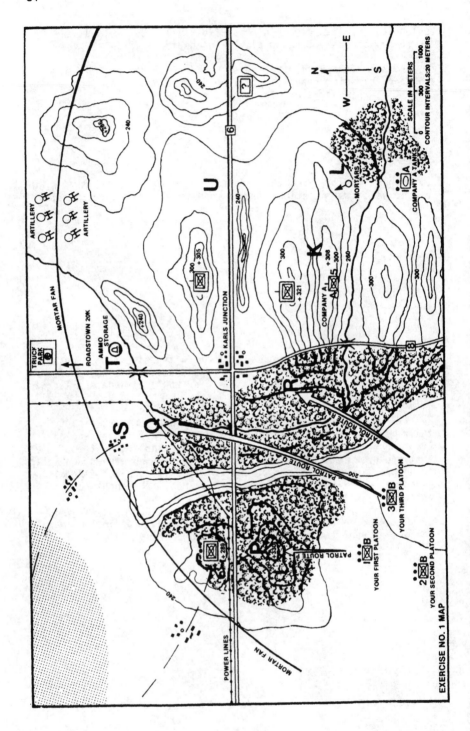

EXERCISE NO. 1 MAP

Solution to Exercise Number 1

Notice the big arc drawn in the north portion of the solution map, extending from the right at about Hill 286, moving left across Hill 240, passing south of the ammunition storage and the bridge, and then arcing up to the northern edge of the map. If you drew your circles or aiming points anywhere north of that line, then you understand something about the concept of surfaces and gaps. You went sufficiently deep, behind enemy lines. You were not afraid to be bold. That is to your credit! There are certainly several correct answers and you should not be too concerned yet over what you circled, so long as it was north of that arc. The optimal choice might be the artillery position and we will come back to the reason for that. For now, rest assured that if you circled anything north of that arc, you are in basic understanding of the concept. Notice the lines in the left portion of the solution map that generally surround Route Q on either side. That represents a gap. If your route went anywhere between those two lines as it proceeded north, once again, you have a basic understanding of the concept of surfaces and gaps.

Why might the artillery be the optimal aiming point, the point to move towards? Because it is something very dear to the enemy. He must have his artillery if he is to suppress us effectively while we are outside the range of his small arms. If he finds that infantry has gotten close in around his artillery, then he has a serious problem and he has to deal with that problem. So in that regard, if we reach his artillery position, we will have disrupted him. We will have seized the initiative and created a problem for him. It appears possible to reach the artillery position, probably from the vicinity of the stream bed.

Some of you may have chosen to seize Hill 286 or Hill 240, seeing them as key terrain from which you might be able to launch an attack on the artillery position. That is certainly acceptable. Your solution is a little more terrain oriented than the artillery position; however, you have gone sufficiently deep to show that you understand the concept of surfaces and gaps. If you circled the ammunition storage, or the truck park, once again, you have selected positions of enemy weakness for your attack. And you have demonstrated a basic understanding of what we are talking about.

Let us now discuss the route that you take from Company B's initial location to whatever you circled north of the arc. Your route, at the time you leave your initial position, is not predictable, because you are going to follow the path of least resistance. You might want to take a route somewhere generally paralleling Route Q because the patrol that arrived at Q reported back that it proceeded along that route without encountering the enemy. Therefore, that route is probably clear. However, you could move out of Company B's position and upon coming alongside of Hill 330 or 289 you might take enemy fire from the left, from out of the woodline that surrounds Hills 330 and 289. If that happened, a correct course of action might be to move into the woodline right of the draw, in there where Patrol Q went. In the event of enemy fire from the left, the concealed route would become the speedier one towards the position you selected north of the arc. That is the route of least resistance. So your actual route would appear to be a zigzagging line. You might even choose to send a unit thrusting out to the left in the manner of Aufrollen, as explained in the discussion of the concept of surfaces and gaps. Do so if it will enhance your speed without dissipating the forces you need for your main effort.

Suppose your main effort is directed toward taking out the enemy's artillery. As long as you keep moving rapidly with forces sufficient to do that, you can send out Aufrollen. Suppose that you went up the draw, embarked in amphibious vehicles and you have found that you were meeting resistance. You might disembark and move through the woods on foot. That might be the speediest route to get up to the artillery position. But, generally, you should move towards that point Q where your recon pull reconnaissance screen was able to get observation of the enemy situation.

Once you arrive at point Q, you may decide not to move directly to the artillery position. If the ammunition storage should be unguarded you may do well to destroy that on the way to the artillery position if you can. However, if you find that the ammunition storage is a strong point, that it has security on it, you might be able to bypass that and in so doing move up to the truck park. The truck park, also, might be a weak spot. If you can destroy the truck park it may be to your advantage to destroy the enemy's mobility and then move into the stream bed from which to launch an attack on the artillery. The goal throughout this is to keep the enemy off balance.

There is also the possibility that you may arrive in the vicinity of the artillery position and find that it has become a strong point because the enemy placed an infantry defense around it during the time your forces were moving. Or the artillery itself may have moved. If the artillery has been reinforced with something that is a threat, you may decide that the aiming point of the attack will be the truck park or the ammunition storage or some new point of vulnerability that has appeared in the enemy's rear, perhaps a command post that has moved in. You want to remain fluid and flexible at all times.

You may wonder why the artillery was chosen as an aiming point in the first place. Artillery is certainly a formidable weapon. But if infantry gets in close around it, the infantry becomes more formidable than the artillery, as far as the artillery is concerned. All things are relative. The artillery must have some kind of security. If you can get inside that security, then you will have the advantage. If you are far out and the artillery has you located, then the enemy has the advantage. You want to move quickly, keep the enemy off balance, keep him from knowing where you are. That is the essence of the concept of surfaces and gaps. That is how it works.

Now, look for a moment at the enemy's situation. Remember, you want him off balance. Remember that you want to put him on the horns of a dilemma. In the scenario, Company A, which was the main effort, initially met enemy resistance when it arrived at Hill 321. Instead of butting its head against the enemy resistance and taking all kinds of casualties, Company A dug in

and the battalion commander shifted the main effort to Company B.
You, as Company B's commander, did not wait for him to designate
you the main effort. You went through the gap without orders.
For the purpose of this problem, assume that your battalion
commander is an expert on the concept of surfaces and gaps. If he
is not, you should not be using this style of warfare. But here,
assume that he and all his company commanders are, indeed,
experts. Company B, using the enormous initiative that
characterizes the subordinate commander in this concept of
surfaces and gaps, moved out on his own without waiting for
orders.

But put yourself for the moment in the shoes of the battalion
commander. Once he becomes aware that this has happened, that
Company B has gone on through a gap, his best option would seem to
be to shift the main effort so that he is indeed pitting strength
against weakness. For company A to continue to be the main effort
and to launch an attack on Hill 321 would be pitting strength
against strength. The battalion commander, if he is familiar with
this concept, would logically say, "I have received a report from
Company B. Company B is on the way to point Q. I will shift the
main effort to Company B." Once he shifts the main effort,
logically, he is going to take the platoon of tanks and send it up
to Company B. He should even take his mortars and send them up to
Company B, because Company B is going to need them. Company A is
going to be dug in and Company A can draw on artillery now,
something slightly less responsive than the mortars. Company A no
longer should have the tanks because its position is static. If
tanks cannot be moving they are not being used to best advantage.
Tanks, mortars, everything possible, goes with the main effort and
the battalion commander, himself, should go with the main effort
to point Q and into the enemy's rear.

The enemy is now on the horns of a dilemma. Look at his
options. He can attack Company A. If he does, he is attacking
the hard spot. He is attacking a surface and he is going to
sustain casualties by doing that. The enemy must decide what to
do about Company B which is running around in his rear. He can
try to guess where Company B is going. Company B is going to be
moving rapidly, being very unpredictable, and that is going to be
difficult. The enemy is likely to perceive incorrectly that
Company B is more than a company. He will really not know what is
going on. So if you can place the enemy in the position of trying
to react to Company B, chasing Company B around, so to speak, you
have very much seized the initiative.

Look further at the enemy's options. He can ignore Company B
and concentrate on Company A. But he cannot ignore Company B for
long because Company B is going to be active in his rear areas.
If he does ignore it he is going to continue to sustain losses.

It would be useful to consider some of the solutions that
students often submit when they are first introduced to this
concept and which could be categorized as difficult-to-defend
solutions. First, consider the patrol at point R. If you got
distracted by that patrol, and sent units out there from Company B
to help it, then you lost speed. You dissipated your forces.

You must ask yourself what the mission is. Your mission is to
enable the most rapid progress to Roadstown. This is a real
problem. You have Marines in trouble and they need help.
However, by continuing on towards the accomplishment of your
mission, you are not letting your Marines down. You are doing
quite the contrary. You are doing your utmost, by moving into the
enemy's rear, to take the pressure off the Marines back in the
vicinity of Hill 321. Remember that this battalion, if it is to
use this style of warfare, must have very strong unit cohesion.
That is one of the things that makes the concept of surfaces and
gaps work. As a cohesive unit, you are confident that your
battalion commander is going to see to it that somebody takes care
of that patrol at point R. So your task is to move without loss
of time and get into the enemy's rear.

I should stop here for a moment and explain myself. I do not
mean to deemphasize the all-important requirement to take care of
our troops. That Marines take care of their own is one of the
mainstays of our esprit. This must always be so. I do wish to
bring to the fore something that we may not emphasize enough. And
that is never lose sight of the mission. That is my point in this
example.

This example is simplified from a real situation. However,
from looking at the responses of students in resident courses, it
is clear that there is a tendency to forget the mission as soon as
the unit begins to take casualties. This is what we will not be
able to do in the next war: Forget the mission. Experience in
combat in Vietnam shows that as soon as a Marine gets hit there is
a tendency among us Americans to forget the mission.

We will take care of our wounded. The mission must come
first. And if we are organized for combat, we will be able,
almost without exception, to take care of our wounded at the same
time that we are accomplishing our mission. Each of us knows that
it is inherent in the duties that we volunteered for as Marines to
risk lives, limbs and the possibility of disfigurement. We have
agreed to take these risks in order to see that our mission,
whatever it may be, is accomplished. No subject that we teach, no
principle that we teach, is more important than that our mission
is to win wars.

Perhaps you decided to attack Hill 321 on the enemy's right
flank, from the west. If you did, you executed what may have
looked like a classic envelopment. However, if you did that, you
certainly would have sustained casualties while taking Hill 321.
Of course you will take casualties no matter what you do. But if
you seize Hill 321 successfully, you are still going to have to
deal with the force on Hill 305 before you are going to be able to
continue your progress on to the north. In other words, you are
not progressing at the most rapid pace possible. You are going
quite slowly. The solution of seizing Hill 321 is not optimal.
Hill 321 is a piece of terrain. That is all it is. It is not of
lasting value to you. Once you get it you are going to have to
leave it. So to get bogged down on Hill 321 would be an incorrect
solution. That is, it would not indicate that you have grasped
the concept of surfaces and gaps. You may have to suppress the
enemy on Hill 321, but Hill 321, itself, is not of lasting value.

Let us say that you looked at your situation and considered the possibility of a flanking attack by Company B on the western part of 321 and then concluded, well, it looks a little shallow for an effective envelopment. You may have wanted to get into the enemy's rear and instead of putting Company B on Hill 321, put it on Hill 305, going in deep. Moving up into the woodline by the stream bed and attacking Hill 305 from a position in the woodline northwest of Karl's Junction, it may have appeared that you would have been enveloping the enemy's right. If you did that, in my opinion, you did not conduct an envelopment at all. The attack you conducted on Hill 305 was a frontal attack. If we accept John Boyd's definition that a flank is "that aspect towards which a force is not directing its primary attention," then you have not found a flank. If you are coming out of the woodline west of Hill 305, the enemy is directing his primary attention towards that woodline, and, therefore, that is his front and not his flank. Always keep in mind that the flank is a relative thing.

If you got preoccupied with the enemy force on Hill 289 (on the left) you do not understand the concept. What is your mission? Your mission is to enable rapid progress towards Roadstown. Don't get sidetracked by small enemy units. Bypass them. Leave them behind. Cut them off from their support. Some of you may have gone around to the right from the eastern part of the mountain where there is an enemy unit shown by a question mark to be of unknown size. If you did that, you are not taking advantage of your reconnaissance screen. You had patrols out at P, Q, and R. They reported facts back. P ran into the enemy. Q got through. R got into serious trouble. Your reconnaissance screen has signalled that the logical thing to do is go through the speedy, unimpeded route. That is Route Q.

There is another reason that your solution must be characterized by speed. Remember that there was some enemy activity observed by the patrol in the vicinity of point S. He saw a few enemy officers and NCOs who appeared to be surveying the terrain. The patrol at Q did not tell you exactly why the enemy was up there. He did not because he did not know. However, you should be able to think through what the patrol did not know. Enemy officers were up there to plan a defensive position for reinforcements that were going to move into the area. Therefore you have got to move fast. If you hesitated, if you did something slow, there is a good possibility that by the time you got up to point Q, that point would be an enemy strong point. But if you move quickly, you can outrun the enemy and get there the firstest with the mostest.

90

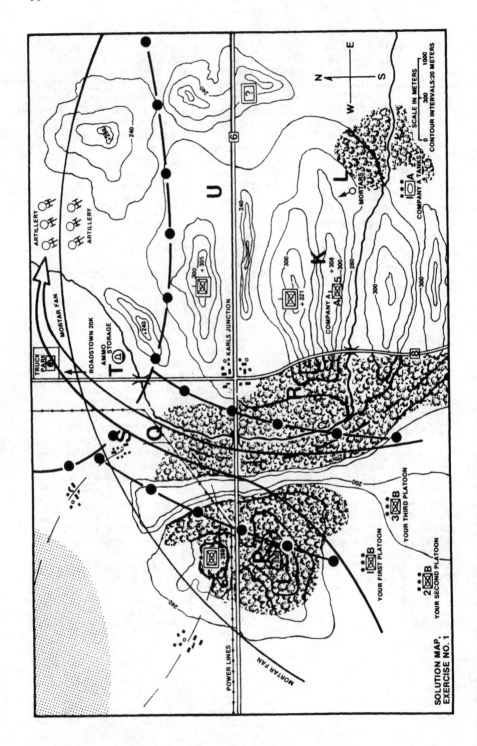

SOLUTION MAP,
EXERCISE NO. 1

Lecture II:
Mission Tactics

The concept of mission tactics, like surfaces and gaps, must always be at work in battle. The name is derived from the German Auftragstaktik, which means, literally, mission tactics. It is no accident that the name includes the word "tactics." Assigning a mission and depending on subordinates to carry it out constitutes the tactic. To allow the subordinate to decide on his own initiative what to do is the means of getting the most appropriate decisions made on the spot and acted on more rapidly than the enemy can respond to your actions.

The subordinate often selects his own objectives or "aiming points." He often has the latitude to decide whether to attack, defend or withdraw. What he must be assigned is the intent or -- in John Boyd's words -- the "output" desired by the commander and a mission.

It is the high degree of initiative allowed the subordinate that gives operations the rapid tempo needed to stay one step ahead of the enemy. When you outpace the enemy in this way, his every decision, by the time he is able to turn it into action, is irrelevant to your action. By the time he reacts, you are already doing something else, something he did not expect.

No course in mission tactics would be complete without relating Moltke's favorite story, told repeatedly in the era of the 1870 war, and recounted most recently by Trevor Depuy in his book, A Genius for War. This is the account of Prince Frederick Charles, who was giving a tongue lashing to one of his majors for committing a tactical blunder. In defense of his action, the major explained that he was only following orders. In the Prussian Army, the major reminded the prince, an order from a senior officer was tantamount to an order from the king. The prince was unimpressed. His reply to the major was, "The King made you a major because he thought you were smart enough to know when not to obey orders."

And that is the essence of mission tactics. The subordinate decides what to do even if it means that the order issued by his senior now should be changed or adjusted. The mission assigned is sacred. The mission is the output that the commander wants. That does not change. But how that output is to be achieved may change, and it is up to the intelligent subordinate to decide whether or not it has.

91

There is a classic example used time and time again in introducing the student to mission tactics. It is simple and of value, so it will be used again here. The subordinate is given the mission of getting his unit across the river. Getting his unit across the river is the output the senior desires. The route that he has been given crosses the nearest bridge. The junior commander arrives at the site to find that the bridge has been destroyed. He does not stop. He does not wait for new orders. He does not request permission to change his route. He goes to the nearest ford several kilometers distant and he crosses there. He informs the senior, of course, as soon as he can. But he does not wait. Remember: Mission orders are necessary to give the tempo of operations the rapidity that it must have if we are to keep the enemy off balance.

It may be useful at this point to compare a mission order against the order that is more typical of slower moving forms of combat. Let us take a situation discussed in the adjoining figure

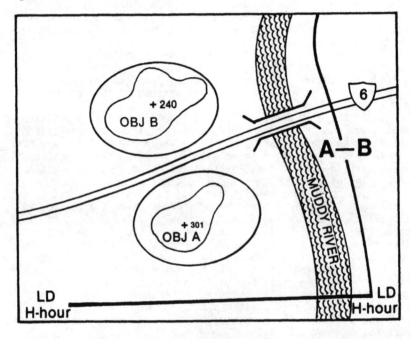

Notice a line of departure. Notice a boundary with Company A on the left and Company B on the right. Our battalion is to cross from the south of the line of departure proceeding north into the zone of action. It is to cross at H hour. Note Objectives A and B on hills 301 and 240, respectively. Let us first take an example from the slower moving form of combat. You are commanding officer, Company A. The battalion's mission is to deny the enemy the use of Route 6, West of the Muddy River. This order is assigned to Company A and it will sound familiar to you, if you have experienced operating in the slower moving form of combat. This order is given to Company A:

"(1) At H hour attack and seize Objective A."
"(2) On order, continue the attack and seize Objective B."
"(3) Establish blocking position to deny the enemy the use of Route 6 West of the Muddy River."

Now consider this order for a moment. You are going to have to attack Objective A whether there is any enemy on the hill or not. You have been ordered to do so. Maybe when the order was issued there was an enemy unit on Objective A. But when you cross the line of departure that may have been changed. In other words, the older style order does not really take into consideration the undeniable fact that the enemy situation is always changing. It does not stay the same. Then, on order, you are to continue the attack and seize Objective B. And, after you do that, then you establish your blocking position. Now that might be exactly what you want to do: proceed in that order. But it might not be, and whether or not it will be the better course of action is entirely unpredictable at the time the order is issued. The enemy will do what he wants to do, not what you want him to do. Unlike an engineer who begins building a bridge, knowing full well that when he finishes the bridge the opposite bank of the river will still be in the position where it was when he began, your situation, as a soldier, is quite different. The only thing you can be certain of is that the opposite bank will not be as it was when you began.

Now look at a mission order. The situation is the same. The adjoining figure still applies. The enemy may or may not be on objectives A or B when the order is issued. Let us say that he has a platoon on each. But, because I, your commander, know that the situation will have changed by the time you cross the line of departure, and because I know that you are smart and you can make your own determination of what to do in order to carry out the assigned mission, I tell you, the commander of Company A, this:

Seize control of Route 6 West of the Muddy River, in order to destroy enemy forces attempting to escape from Company B's zone of action.

This allows you to proceed at your own pace. Naturally, you are going to proceed at as rapid a pace as you possibly can. You make the determination what is possible. You are not going to throw your forces away. But, if you find Objectives A and B are clear or that you can suppress the enemy on them you may want to bypass them. You know that you are there to destroy enemy forces attempting to escape from Company B's zone of action. Maybe you can do that best on the road. Maybe you discover that there is a ford across the Muddy River and the road becomes meaningless. You know why you are there.

Notice in the mission order the phrase, "in order to." That is a very important phrase and usually ought to go in the mission order. There is no rule that every mission order contain the phrase, "in order to." If you were told, "attack that enemy company that you see in front of you," it would probably be highly superfluous to tell you why. They are there, they are a threat, why waste the breath? But usually your mission order will have the ability to endure <u>time</u> better if you explain to your subordinate <u>why</u> he is carrying the mission out: "In order to--." This gives the order the quality that Erich von Manstein called "long-term." It can endure the test of time. Your commander can lose communication with you yet you can still carry out his intent because you know what he wanted and you can continue to act within his intent for a long time without checking back.

Before leaving the subject of whether or not the phrase "in order to" should be in every mission order, it is appropriate to dwell for a moment on the subject of formats and content. "In order to" is handy, but it would be awkward to establish a rule requiring the phrase's constant use. It has been said, "the art of war has no traffic with rules," and this is very valid. Especially when we are dealing with professionals, well schooled in the art of war, there is all the less reason to make them follow fixed rules. Fixed rules are not appropriate in instructing how to assign missions. Too often, students reject good ideas about tactics because they cannot get their thoughts to fit the format of the operation order that is being demanded. The important thing is that the mission be clear. Compared to clarity, format is of little or no consequence.

FMFM 3-1, the Marine Corps Manual on Command Staff Action, says at one point that the mission assigned must contain the "who, where, when and so much of the why as necessary for intelligence coordination and cooperation." Even this rule is too structured. Take, for instance, the requirement to specify the when of a mission. If you are told the time to attack, constraints have been placed on you. Sometimes a time schedule is convenient in combat for the sake of coordination. Often, however, a time schedule builds rigidity into your operations. Your operations cannot be based on a clock. They must be based on the enemy. The enemy will never comply with your time schedule. This is just one example of why it is awkward and even sometimes dangerous to be too stringent about formats in the giving of orders.

Another guideline for using mission orders is to give orders by word of mouth whenever possible. Do not depend on written orders. At one time, General Hermann Balck, Commander of the German 11th Panzer Division in World War II, strictly forbade written orders in his division. His instructions were, "All orders will be verbal!" He probably gave this instruction out of frustration over the clumsiness of too many written orders. It became the German practice to issue orders by word of mouth, execute the operations, and later on, when there was time, write the orders down for the record. They recognized that written orders are slow and cumbersome.

Balck's practice when preparing for a dawn attack was to assemble his subordinate commanders the evening before and give detailed orders verbally and personally. It was important that he have face to face contact when he issued these initial orders to avoid any possible misunderstanding. Then after his subordinates returned to their units, when the time came to move out, General Balck would pass by radio or telephone the message, "no change to orders," unless the enemy situation had developed in such a way that there should be a change. Then he would pass by radio or telephone the change only.

In this way, he kept his orders brief and the tempo of his operations fast. One of General Balck's favorite sayings was, "Don't work hard, work fast." So you can see the extreme importance that this great commander attached to speed. After the initial order, based upon which his forces went into action, all subsequent orders could be extremely brief.

Sometimes the initial order can be brief. In fact, contrary to what is often believed, initial orders at smaller unit levels must be longer and more detailed than those at division, corps and army levels. How often we take the opposite approach! Once these initial lengthier orders are issued, however, if they are well formed, all subsequent orders in the course of combat can be extremely brief. And there will be little need for many subsequent orders, if any are required at all.

At first glance, this may look very simple. It may look as if it relieves the senior commander of burdens of responsibility. Much of the decision-making will be done by subordinates. But on studying the concept more closely, you will find that it requires more skill, more talent and more professionalism on the part of any commander to operate with mission orders. The commander must be better able to articulate what is to be the output. As you begin to do exercises you will find how difficult it can be to express exactly what you want done. But the accomplished commander can do this well and it comes through practice. You will have the opportunity to practice this in the exercises at the end of this lecture. In classroom exercises you should constantly be asked, "What orders do you give now?" Through practice you will learn to respond quickly and clearly.

The other side of the coin is that the subordinate receiving the order must be more talented. Amateur troops, awkward, clumsy, untrained troops, cannot be expected to carry out mission orders. Why? Because as a result of their lack of experience they must be told what to do. Only the professional, the experienced leader, can know what to do without being told. Because we in the Marine Corps set our standards high, we expect that our subordinates will train until they can perform under mission orders. We will set our standard at that level and work up to it.

Burdens of responsibility increase on both sides; on the part of the senior commander and on the part of the subordinate. Look first at the senior commander. Operating with mission orders, his orders must be perfectly clear. The onus is on the senior to define to the junior what must be accomplished without telling him how to do it. The onus is not on the junior to ferret out what his commander wants. The senior must state what he wants. Otherwise, he should not expect to get it.

In the early 1960's at The Basic School when lieutenants were instructed in the five-paragraph order and how to carry it out, great emphasis was placed on having received the mission, deciding what was the specified mission or missions, and what were implied missions. In other words, the junior was expected to ferret out what the senior wanted. This should not be necessary. The senior should make it perfectly clear what is wanted.

An additional burden of responsibility on the senior is that he must train his subordinates and his unit to operate as a team. They are not going to be able to perform mission orders without training.

Another new burden of responsibility is that he must expect his subordinates to make mistakes; he may not expect "zero defects." Wars are won by people, not machines. People make mistakes. If people are more afraid of making mistakes than they are of exercising initiative now and then, they will not take risks and they will not exercise initiative. Furthermore, they will not win in war.

Perhaps the most important new responsibility that is placed on the commander who gives the mission orders is that he must trust his subordinates. If trust breaks down the whole system breaks down.

This even provides some insight into the question that recurs: Why did the Germans lose World War II? After 1942, after Stalingrad, Hitler relieved talented generals, actually taking personal command, himself, of a field army group. In other words, trust broke down, and this was felt through the chain of command so that finally the smooth, well-oiled machine stopped working. Adolph Hitler in World War II is a good example of one who stopped trusting his commanders. So trust broke down.

You can see a similar phenomenon under Napoleon. In the earlier days his tactics were very fluid. The Grand Armee worked as a team. But after it got into Russia it began to get sticky. It no longer worked smoothly. Trust broke down. Napoleon stopped trusting his marshals. (Well he should have, some were plotting his assassination).

So trust is extremely important. Trust up and trust down. In order to operate with mission order tactics, the commander must be sure that he informs his subordinates not only of their mission but of his mission and the mission next above him. This is known as the "two echelons up rule." Each commander must be fully aware of the mission two echelons up.

Now look at the new responsibility that the subordinate incurs with mission orders. The "two echelon up" rule is a good place to start. The platoon commander cannot run his platoon without knowing full well what the battalion commander is trying to do. Likewise, of course, he must know what the company commander is trying to do. If he is ignorant of the desired outputs of the two commanders above him, there will be times when he will have to ask what to do, or guess what to do, or wait for orders, all of which will slow down the process which is tactics. The company commander must think into the mind not only of his battalion commander but the regimental commander. The battalion commander must be read into the thoughts and desires of the division commander.

Above all else, with mission orders, junior officers, non-commissioned officers, and troops must use initiative. Once the subordinate receives his mission he takes it from there. He does not wait for orders. And he must not lose sight of the main effort. He must be well aware of what the main effort is.

The main effort will be the subject of the next concept under study, which must be thoroughly understood in order to perform faster moving combat.

EXERCISE NUMBER 2

MISSION TACTICS

<u>PART I</u>

1. You are Commanding Officer, Company A, 1st Tank Battalion.
You are attached to 1st Battalion, 5th Marine Regiment. Your
chain of command is shown below. It is 0900 on 22 September
1981.

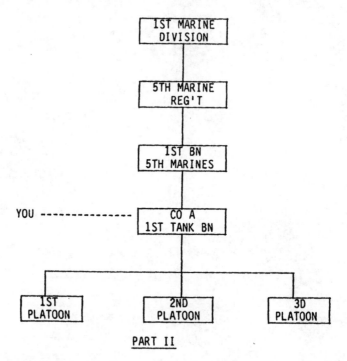

<u>PART II</u>

1. Refer to Map #1. You know that an enemy company is on Hill
368. Another is on Hill 311. The two enemy companies are
supported by a company of tanks, as shown on Map #1. Their
mission appears to be to deny us the use of the Route 8 bridge
over the Muddy River, a well-constructed bridge that could support
our tanks as well as the enemy's. The Muddy River can be forded
by tanks and crossed by amphibious assault vehicles (AAV's),
however, its muddy banks will make such operations slow and
unpredictable. Wheeled vehicles cannot cross except at the
bridge. The 5th Regiment has with it a company of amphibious
assault vehicles which are all with the 1st Battalion (enough
vehicles to lift the entire battalion) in order to enable your
battalion's rifle companies to enjoy a high degree of mobility.
All logistic support units as well as the preponderance of the

division's men and equipment are dependent upon wheeled or foot mobility. The 2d Battalion is the regiment's "main effort" battalion. It is completely heliborne. Its objective is to "seize the north bank of the Muddy River."

2. You know that the 5th Marines' mission is as follows:

Establish a secure bridgehead across the Muddy River. Conduct offensive and defensive operations in order to protect the bridge until all 1st Marine Division units have crossed the Muddy River.*

3. The regiment has chosen a crossing point about 10K west from the left edge of your map. The crossing point is not occupied by the enemy.

4. You know that 1st Battalion, 5th Marines has this mission:

Attack enemy forces that are on the south side of the Muddy River, in order to deceive the enemy into thinking that our objective is the Route 8 bridge.

5. Your mission was stated to you as follows:

Attack and disrupt the enemy on Hill 368 without becoming decisively engaged. After the division's river crossing is successful break contact, cross the Muddy by most expeditious route available, rejoin the regiment and continue movement to Roadstown.

6. The concept of operations calls for Second Battalion to helilift to positions north of the Muddy as the Third Battalion, on the south side, protects the efforts of engineers to construct a bridge at night. The main effort of the regiment is that of the Second Battalion, whose task it is to secure the northern bank of the river.

7. Your attack is to begin at 1400 on 22 September.

PART III

1. It is now 1400, 22 September. Your tanks roll over Hill 355 and begin to fire on Hill 368. But there are no targets. There is no return fire. The enemy is no longer there.

2. The situation is now as shown on Map #2.

*This does not mean that one bridgehead is the only crossing point that the division will use. It merely means that the division commander wants a secure bridge available until his division is across the river.

3. The enemy, having located 1st Battalion, moved off his position in full force, joined reinforcements and is concentrating all his combat power against 1st Battalion. You are out of communication with 1st Battalion.

4. The noises of intense ground and air combat are heard on your right.

5. A message does get through from Second Battalion (remember that they were to make the heli-lift north of the river). The message is as follows:

> Second Battalion has not crossed the river. Enemy air strikes destroyed friendly helicopters. There will be no heli-lift. Second Battalion proceeding north on Route 8 by motor transport with rubber boats. We should arrive at [Point R on map 2] in one hour. Will effect surface crossing.

6. Third battalion will arrive at its crossing point, 10 K west from the left edge of your map, at 2000. Bridge construction originally planned to begin at 2000 may be delayed six hours because of destruction of equipment caused by the air attack.

PART IV

STUDENT REQUIREMENTS

1. State briefly (only in the space provided) what is your decision (purpose and main effort).

2. With your green pen circle any area or areas to which you will initially send your unit or units, as you would in designating a terrain objective.

3. Draw green arrows from the locations of your three platoons to the points you intend to send them, showing their general routes.

4. State below one mission that you, as company commander, assign to one of your platoons. You may pick any one of your three platoons. You need not, in this exercise, write out the mission of the other two platoons. In the interest of time, write only one well thought out, clearly stated mission of quality.

101

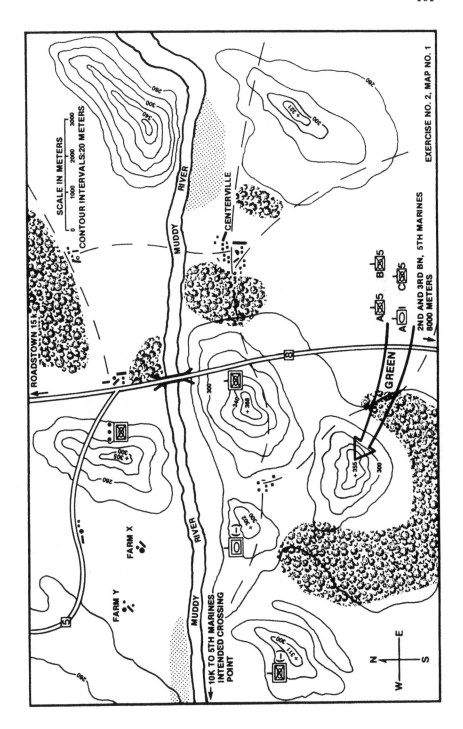

SCALE IN METERS

0 1000 2000 3000

CONTOUR INTERVALS:20 METERS

EXERCISE NO. 2, MAP NO. 1

ROADSTOWN 15 k

MUDDY RIVER

CENTERVILLE

MUDDY RIVER

FARM X

FARM Y

10K TO 5TH MARINES
INTENDED CROSSING
POINT

GREEN

A☒5   B☒5
A⬡   C☒5

2ND AND 3RD BN, 5TH MARINES
8000 METERS

N
W   E
S

102

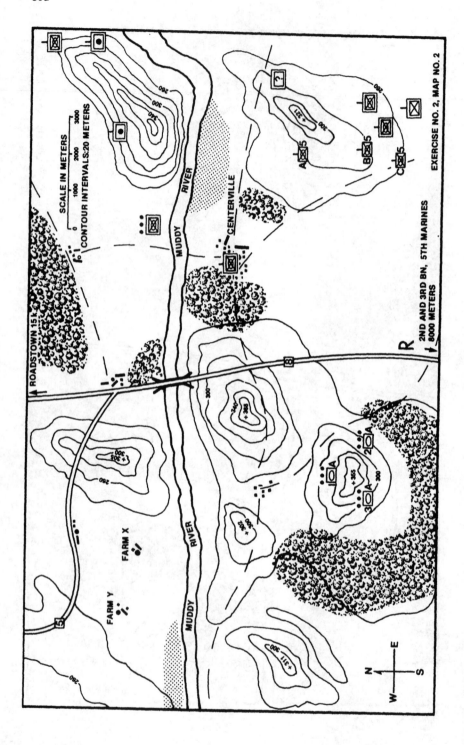

SCALE IN METERS

0   1000   2000   3000

CONTOUR INTERVALS: 20 METERS

EXERCISE NO. 2, MAP NO. 2

2ND AND 3RD BN, 5TH MARINES

8000 METERS

Solution to Exercise Number 2

In my solution to Exercise Number 2, I drew three separate aiming points, one for each tank platoon. The first was on Hill 305 itself. The second was drawn to the first village west of Hill 305 and the third to the second village west of Hill 305. If your aiming points were anywhere north of the Muddy River, then you get credit for putting them in the right place.

This route goes across the bridge. All three platoons will attempt to cross the bridge. The reason is that that is the speediest route. Tactics here must be fluid. Perhaps in getting the first platoon across, the effort will be detected and the bridge will come under fire from the east. War is unpredictable! If that happens, success will depend on the <u>initiative</u> of the second and third platoon commanders. On their own, they should veer off to the west and cross the Muddy somewhere west of the bridge. Their crossing points <u>they</u> will select. The chances are that they will not follow one in tandem of the other if the bridge comes under fire. They would fan out and get across the river as quickly as possible somewhere west of the bridge. But that is a decision the platoon commanders make. It is a decision that their commander cannot make for them. They know where he wants them to arrive in the end. They know what he wants them to do.

Look at the mission order given to the first platoon. It says, "Cross to the north of the Muddy River rapidly and take positions, reference Hill 305, in order to engage enemy forces as necessary to enable the earliest crossing of other 1st Marine Division units." Now he knows why he is there. And he makes the decisions. He knows he should be somewhere in the vicinity of Hill 305, not necessarily on it. The other platoons have general locations and they have been ordered to cross the Muddy River rapidly, first platoon having priority to cross the bridge first.

North of the river, Second and Third platoons are to revert to company reserve. Second platoon is assigned to the vicinity Farm X. In the case of the Third platoon, the vicinity Farm Y. They have specific places to go because they are in the reserve. They belong to the company commander. As his reserve, they have a little less independence than they will have once committed. This will be discussed further under the concept of the Reserve.

First platoon is committed. He has full latitude to make decisions and act within the mission assigned to him, without waiting for orders. The company commander is going to be with the First Platoon. He will be there ready to deal with the enemy. As the company commander, his reserve is his main means for dealing with the enemy, once First platoon develops the situation. He will be up front so we will know how and when to employ the reserve.

Invariably, students are surprised by this approach to the problem. Some would instead immediately go after the enemy north of the River. This approach is different. Some say the initiative has been ceded to the enemy. Not so. Not anymore than Napoleon ceded the initiative at Austerlitz. The company has stopped north of the river and if it appears to the enemy that he

has the initiative then that is fine. Let him attack. He doesn't
know where the reserves are. They are poised ready to resume the
offensive as soon as possible. All the force need not be
concentrated at this point. It is best to disperse until we
engage. We will fight concentrated once the enemy comes into a
position where he is a threat to us. (Remember Rommel's maxim:
"move dispersed, fight concentrated"). But we want to keep that
bridge, if possible, so we can get the division across as early as
possible. From this standpoint the tank company should not be
running off to the east where those enemy forces are north of the
Muddy from 1st Battalion, 5th Marines. It should not run off
after those artillery positions because if it does, it leaves the
bridge completely uncovered.

If you did go off after the artillery positions, your solution
is still acceptable. If you went after the artillery, at least
you took the initiative. You made a decision. You crossed the
river. You were bold.

If you chose to leave some forces south of the river, then you
dissipated your forces. You really did not make up your mind what
to do. Many students have problems with this. They want to leave
somebody on the other side of the bridge. If you do that, you are
falling into the trap of the amateur. That is, you are trying to
"cover all the bases."

Consider for a moment the south side of the bridge. What can
happen there? There is an enemy motorized rifle company in
Centerville. And many students fancy that company coming to the
south end of the bridge and defending there if we do not leave
some of our own tanks back to prevent that from happening.

But that company is not likely to move very far, very fast.
They will probably think that you did leave somebody to "cover all
the bases" and if they approach the south end of the bridge at
all, they will do so cautiously. They will not assume that you
left it naked. You need all your forces on one side of the river
so that youcan fight your company as a company, with one up and
two back. Because if you fight, you fight to win. You do not
want the company spread with part of it on one side of the river
and part of it on the other. You want the whole thing where you
can fight and win a quick victory.

There is another reason the company in Centerville is not
likely to go for the bridge. Look at the enemy situation. He is
closing in on 1st Battalion, 5th Marines. He does not have any-
body providing any kind of security between him and his forces
north of the Muddy except the company in Centerville. That enemy
company in Centerville has a mission. Here it is best to gamble
and bet that the enemy company in Centerville is not at liberty to
go traipsing off to the south side of the bridge. He has a mis-
ion in Centerville. He is going to stay there and carry it out.
Remember, the enemy is not as fluid as you are and he is not as
smart as you. You should try to predict what he is going to do.

Some students worry that if they do not have somebody sitting
there on the bridge, the enemy is going to go and blow the bridge
up. That does not seem likely. The enemy needs the bridge more
than you do. After all, it is his forces who have extended
themselves with a small portion of them on one side of the river

while their reserves and reinforcements are up on the north of the river. He needs the bridge more than you do. He will be reluctant to destroy it.

One more point favors the case for taking the whole company across the river. Second battalion is coming up as indicated on your map. If they get there and there is an enemy company at the bridge, it is the enemy company that is going to lose. So even if they do defend the bridge, they are going to be destroyed in the long run. The best bet is to go ahead, seize the bridge, get it in friendly hands by getting a goodly force, that is the whole company of tanks, north of the bridge where it can fight for the bridgehead there.

Remember these are fluid tactics. You are not going to hold terrain. You are defending the bridge but that does not mean that you are going to sit on Hill 305; nor does it mean that you are going to sit on the bridge; nor does it mean that you are going to sit in the woodline north of the bridge. All those are territory to move through and around to fight the enemy. Defending the bridge is not defending terrain. You may go as far as the woodline 3,000 meters northeast of the bridge.

As noted earlier, some of you may even have chosen to go to the enemy artillery position on the hill to the east. If you did you are still defending the bridge. You will have great difficulty, however, in justifying your action if you dissipated your forces. Likewise, you are on shaky ground if you went back to 1st Battalion, 5th Marines. 1st Battalion is having to fight. But the battalion's mission is to enable that division to get across the river. And for you to do anything that would slow the division down would be to jeopardize that mission.

106

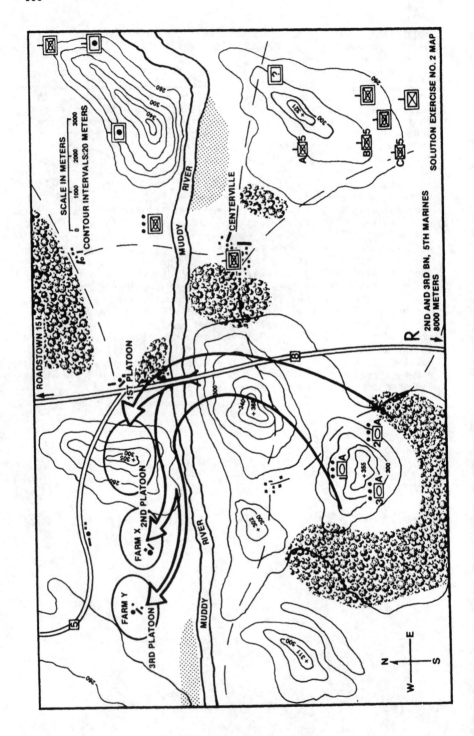

Lecture III:
The Main Effort

The commander, in making his plan, must determine what and where his main effort is in every operation, whether it be offensive, defensive or withdrawal. This main effort should be specified in the operation order. It should always be clearly stated in paragraph 3a, The Concept of Operations.

There can only be one main effort. When you start giving two or three or a three part main effort, you had better look back at it because the chances are you have not made up your mind what you are trying to do.

Every unit commander down to the company commander will always assign a main effort and sometimes even the platoon commander should. The company commander will assign the main effort to one of his platoons. The battalion commander will assign it to one of his companies, the regimental commander to one of his battalions. This platoon, company or battalion that is assigned the main effort may be reinforced. It could even be two companies, but, generally, it should be assigned to a single element. The main effort is supported by the entire command.

Think for a moment at the regimental level. The regimental commander assigns a main effort to a battalion. The entire regiment, everything that belongs to that regiment, will support that battalion. Let us say it is the 1st Battalion. I, as the regimental commander, will give that battalion the benefit of everything I have. I will give them the benefit of my tanks, my artillery and my logistic support. I will give them the benefit of my air. That does not mean that all these arms will be attached to the main effort battalion. They may be, if appropriate. But they will be doing things that support what that main effort battalion commander is doing. The main effort battalion should receive priority on mobility: trucks, helicopters and everything else that helps him move.

The entire command must be aware of what and where the main effort is. The commander can change the main effort at any time. This is what gives the operation its fluidity.

Here are a few examples of how the main effort works. Most of these historical examples, in fact all of them, will come from the Germans. It is not out of any particular love for the Germans, but because only the Germans had this concept and used it

consistently in their tactics. You could find plans and
operations of other countries that seemed to encompass the use of
a main effort but it would be grasping for likenesses of main
efforts, trying to make main efforts out of things that were not
conceived as such. Since the Germans are the ones who developed
the concept and used it consciously, it is only logical that the
main effort be demonstrated from German operations.

The German word for the main effort is _Schwerpunkt_. Anytime
in your readings when you see that, and often you will see it
written in italics, the German word, _Schwerpunkt_, take note
because it is one of the most important and underlying concepts in
everything the Germans do.

One of the clearest historical examples of the _Schwerpunkt_, or
main effort, can be seen in the battle of France in 1940. This of
course is a strategic example but, as such, it is one about which
you can find a good deal of source material to read and reread
until you understand. You can apply the concept quite as well at
the operational or the small unit tactical level.

Consider then the German invasion of France in World War II.
The initial plan devised by the high command was to attack through
the low countries, Belgium and the Netherlands. They would
conduct subsidiary actions in the south through the Ardennes
mountains. That is, the main effort would be to the north, or to
the right, through the low countries. Secondary efforts would be
on the left. This was precisely what was planned for World War I
in accordance with the Schlieffen plan.

Because it was a repeat of a plan that had previously been
tried and that had previously failed, some German generals did not
like the idea, in particular Erich von Manstein. He argued
strongly that the _Schwerpunkt_ should not be on the right.
Manstein was convinced that the enemy would expect the attack to
come through the low countries. The avenues of approach were
better there. There were more roads. The Germans could move more
quickly, it would seem. But, because they would be expected by
the enemy, Manstein argued progress would in fact be slowed if not
stopped by enemy action. Manstein also realized that the enemy
thought that a major tank attack through the Ardennes would be
impossible. In the Ardennes, Manstein supposed that the enemy
would be weak. There they could surprise the enemy; therefore,
that should be the main effort.

Manstein persevered to overcome many objections. Finally, he
convinced Hitler that the main effort should be on the left. It
worked. They attacked through the Ardennes. They put their
strength there, sending seven of their ten Panzer divisions
through the Ardennes which it was thought would be impossible for
tanks to traverse. The remainder of their forces went through the
low countries and the British and French went to meet them there.
In other words, the enemy strength was on the German right which
was not their main effort. The German left, which continued to be
the main effort, punched through enemy weakness, completely
disrupting the French and British armies. They overran France in
six weeks.

Consider this same thing on the tactical level. Make the main
effort where the enemy least expects you. Make the main effort

where the enemy is weak. But be prepared to be surprised. Be leery of the counsel, "Do not ever be suprised." In war you will be surprised. The task is to learn to deal with surprise. If what you thought would be enemy weakness becomes enemy strength, you should not be disrupted. If your tactics are fluid you can deal with surprise. You will shift your main effort to enemy weakness and go on through. That is how the main effort works in the offense.

Remember, every operation must have a main effort. Never say "This is the approach march, there is no main effort." Never say "This is the defense, this is the withdrawal, so no main effort is needed." Always there is a main effort and that main effort reflects what you are trying to do. For instance, "Attack through the Ardennes and proceed to the English Channel; therefore, main effort is such-and-such Panzer corps."

The main effort should be directed against enemy weakness, not enemy strength. Here you see the interconnection between the concepts, the connection between the concept of the main effort and the concept of surfaces and gaps. All the concepts work together at the same time. The main effort cannot be understood in isolation from surfaces and gaps because it is directed against enemy weakness.

Say that in our ever-changing enemy situation on the battle-field you direct your main effort at a point of enemy weakness and suddenly the enemy reinforces there so that what was a point of enemy weakness becomes a point of enemy strength. At this time, the main effort should be shifted to a new point. If Company A, as the main effort, struck enemy strength, and it cannot be with-drawn easily, the solution would be to designate another company, perhaps Company B, as the new main effort and have it pass through a point of enemy weakness. In so doing, the enemy, forced to react, may well take the pressure off of Company A. This gives the battlefield fluidity. Because the battalion commander has the latitude to make changes like this on his own without permission, he is also applying the concept of mission tactics. So, again you see an interconnection between the concepts. They work together.

Consider the defense. The commander will decide where he thinks the enemy will attack. He will try to read himself into the mind of the enemy and determine where it is logical the enemy will go. He can only do this if he studies closely the character-istics of his opponent.

He designates a main effort based on what he expects his enemy to do. Again, his tactics are fluid. All things in war are unpredictable. If the enemy does not come where you want him to come, we must be prepared to shift the main effort, but there will always be a main effort.

Some of this sounds very alien to the American concept of defense. In 1953 German General Franz Halder completed a critique of the U. S. Army Tactical Doctrine. The item he was most critical of was American understanding of the defense. He read the Army Field Manual 100-5 and saw where it said that the defense is used only to gain time, to regroup before going back on the offensive, or to hold terrain. He said the Americans do not understand what the defense is for. The defense is another way of getting at the enemy. It is another way of destroying him.

Therefore, choose a main effort. Study how Napoleon went on the defensive at Austerlitz to draw his enemy in and render one of the most decisive defeats in history. After the battle, Napoleon, in the exuberance of victory, said, "It seemed that I was in command of both armies!" His enemy had fallen for his trap perfectly.

See on the diagram where the commander has decided to make his left appear to be a weak spot. He will try to draw the enemy in there. The enemy has two alternatives here. He may enter through the weak spot on our left or he may attack the hard spot on our right. Either will get him into trouble. If he attacks the hard spot on the right, he is attacking a dug-in, fortified enemy and he will sustain casualties. If he goes through the weak spot he has been drawn into our trap. Of course if he attacks the hard spot we will try to use fluid tactics, change the main effort, and make that be a trap too.

Let us now presume that he attacks on our left. In so doing, he exposes his flank to us. Once he does that we designate the reserve the main effort and commit it as shown.

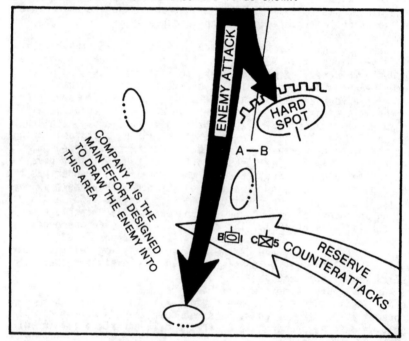

Of course you will have more than one plan for committing the reserve, but the example shows one way that the reserve can be used to come in for the decisive blow. So a large reserve is something which always must be held in offensive or defensive combat and it should, when committed, support or become the main effort.

Though German examples have been used here, the main effort is not something alien to other peoples' forms of warfare, though usually in other armies it is less clearly defined. Consider our own principles of war, which we got from the British in the 1920s, and you will see vestiges of the main effort in them.

Consider the principle of the objective. Remember, the main effort is where you determine you are going to do something decisive. That should be what you do when you select an objective. Therefore, there is a relationship.

Consider the principle of mass. The Germans put seven of their ten Panzer divisions in the main effort on a narrow front and left the other three on the broader front to the right. But they massed their forces against enemy weakness with the main effort. Mass is one of our U. S. Army's principles of war and when Nathan Bedford Forrest said, "Get thar fustest with the mostest," he was saying something about the principle of mass.

The principle of economy of force is also there in the main effort. Your assets are always going to be limited. Therefore, decide what you are going to do and use your assets to best effect by placing them where they will do the most good, against enemy weakness. That way you preserve your assets. You do not dissipate them and lose them by throwing them against enemy strength.

Even the principle of simplicity can be recognized in the concept of the main effort. Instead of trying to do ten different things, we are focusing on one. There will be many other efforts going on at the same time but all in some way directed at making the main effort succeed.

So what do you gain from this main effort? You gain direction. You gain fluidity. You gain speed. And you prevent dissipating your efforts all over the battlefield, the way the Poles did when the Germans invaded Poland. They tried to defend their entire 800-mile front. There was no main effort and by trying to be strong everywhere they were in fact strong nowhere. This trying to "cover all the bases" is a common error in the amateur commander's plan. It is a symptom of avoidance of decision-making.

By establishing a main effort, you make a clear decision. You obviate the necessity for juniors to keep asking for guidance. If they know their commander's main effort, they can continue to operate even though communications may be cut, and they can continue to operate at a high tempo because they need not keep checking back for new orders.

Also, by always having a main effort, you provide an answer to those who worry that with the concepts of surfaces and gaps and mission tactics forces will be straying willy-nilly about the battlefield. They are not doing so because they know what the main effort is. A photograph of their activities from an airplane might appear to be a picture of willy-nilly movement about the battlefield. It is, in fact, nothing of the kind. If it appears shapeless and thereby confuses the enemy, that is very good. Every subordinate knows his commander's intent and his mission. Every subordinate knows his commander's main effort and he makes his decisions based on those three things.

You will be given exercises in which you will be required to select your main effort. You must do exercises in which you are required to choose your main effort <u>quickly</u> and shift it quickly. You should always be able to respond succinctly and definitively to the question, "What is your main effort right now?" That answer should be very brief. Your mission order may be longer. It may have the phrase, "in order to." It will show <u>why</u> such-and-such a unit is your main effort. But the main effort is succinct. "My main effort is 1st platoon; my main effort is 3rd battalion." The unit you designate and its mission are the focus of your effort.

When the commander has made this decision he has done something very necessary. He has done something very ethical. He has assumed and taken responsibility. For what will happen if the battle goes awry? He cannot blame his subordinates. He can only blame himself. It was he who decided what was to be done and designated a main effort in order to do it. Therefore, it takes courage and moral character to select a main effort. That is why the weak commander and the amateur so often fail to do this. In fact, the weak commander will actively avoid choosing a main effort. It is very convenient for the commander weak in character to avoid selecting a main effort because, if the battle goes unfavorably, he can blame someone else for the mistake. The commander who has taken a stand and selected his own main effort cannot do this. Therefore, in this sense, the main effort is a moral commitment.

The main effort underlies everything you do in battle. If I were asked to select any of these concepts as the most important, the main effort, <u>Schwerpunkt</u>, is that which I would select. Von Hindenburg made the statement: "Battle without a <u>Schwerpunkt</u> is like a man without character." The main effort is the most important element and the only element that gives the battle focus.

Exercise Number 3

MAIN EFFORT

PART I

1. You are the Commanding Officer, Company A, reinforced with one platoon of tanks (5 tanks) and an anti-tank section (8 TOW wire-guided missiles) and a platoon of AAV's (enough to lift everyone). Your chain of command is shown below. It is 1500 22 September 1981.

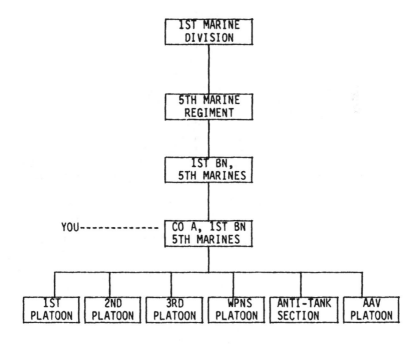

PART II

1. Your regiment (5th Marines) has seized Roadstown. The enemy continues to resist by all remaining means. In order to exploit a wide gap found in the enemy's defenses, your battalion, i.e., 1st Battalion, 5th Marines has been committed as part of the reserve. You have attacked through the gap and into the heart of the enemy's position.

2. You know that your regiment's mission is:

Seize control of Roadstown logistic base in order to force the enemy's main force* to fight on terrain of our choosing,

disrupt his communications, and deny him the use of the
Roadstown rail heads.

3. You know that your battalion's mission is:

Attack enemy forces in the north Roadstown suburban sector in
order to destroy their ability to continue resistance.

4. Your unit has been designated the main effort of the
battalion. You have been assigned a zone of action, which is
represented by the entirety of your exercise map. Your mission
was stated as follows:

Attack enemy forces in your zone of action in order to destroy
their ability to continue resistance.

5. Because you represent the battalion's main effort, the
remainder of the battalion is supporting you, and in so doing, is
providing protection to your flanks and rear so that you can
proceed with your mission. Because the battalion is committed in
this manner, you cannot plan on a large reserve from battalion
coming to your assistance.

6. On surveying the enemy situation shown on Map #1, you should
look carefully for enemy vulnerabilities. There are many. They
result from your unit having broken through to a position where
you are not supposed to be (as far as the enemy is concerned).

7. This exercise is to test your understanding of the main
effort.

*The main force is to the east 50K from Roadstown, moving rapidly
towards 5th Marines' position.

PART III

Proceed according to the following steps:

1. Refer to EXERCISE KEY III. You will be required to reproduce
with your green pen the four arrows shown in the exercise key.
Draw your arrows approximately the same size as those shown in the
key. In part IV of the exercise you will have the opportunity to
draw symbols inside the arrows representing your TOW Section, 60mm
Mortar Section, Machine Gun Section, and Assault Section. Draw
the arrows so that they point to the target you wish to strike.
As an exercise in discipline and decision-making you may only use
each symbol one time.

2. Now draw in the "Main Effort" arrow.

3. Now draw in the "Pinning Force" arrow.

4. Now draw in the Reserve Position.

*5. Now draw in and label the "Artillery Suppression" arrow.

*6. Now draw in and label the "Air Strike" arrow. Remember that air will be available to support your main effort. The air target that you designate with your arrow should strike somewhere other than the point of your main effort.

*Because of limited resources you may strike only one target apiece with these arrows. You may, if you wish, place both on the same target, or the target engaged by your pinning force, or your main effort force.

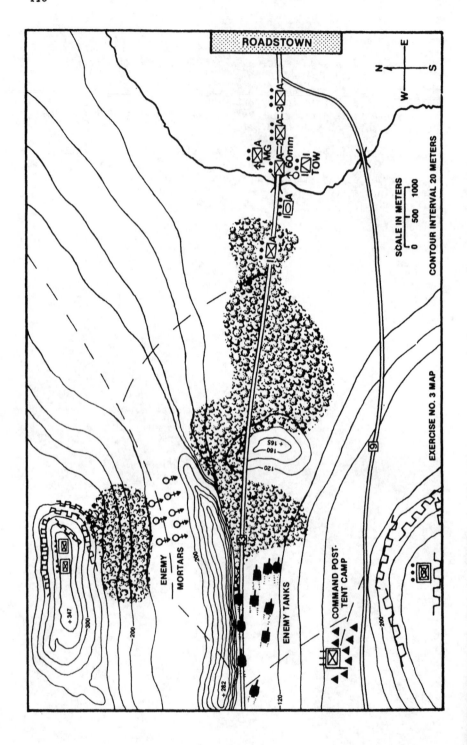

ROADSTOWN

SCALE IN METERS

0   500   1000

CONTOUR INTERVAL 20 METERS

EXERCISE NO. 3 MAP

ENEMY
MORTARS

ENEMY TANKS

COMMAND POST-
TENT CAMP

EXERCISE KEY III

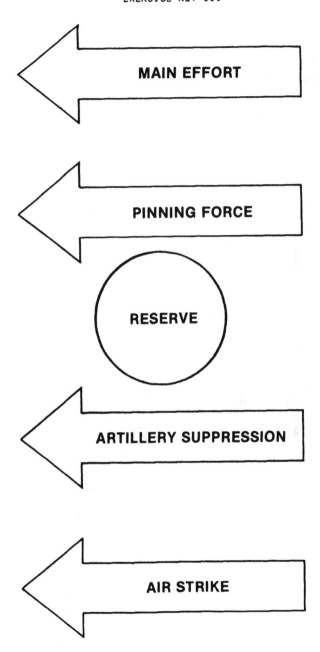

PART IV

Proceed according to the following steps:

1. Refer to EXERCISE KEY IV. You will be required to reproduce with your green pen the symbols shown. If the unit is to come under the command of the main effort, place it within his arrow. If the unit is to come under the command of the pinning force, place it within his arrow. If a unit is to be part of the reserve, place it within the reserve position. If the unit is to come directly under your command, do not place it inside an arrow but show it at approximately the location that you intend for it to be. If you plan to split any of the sections, you need not depict them at all.

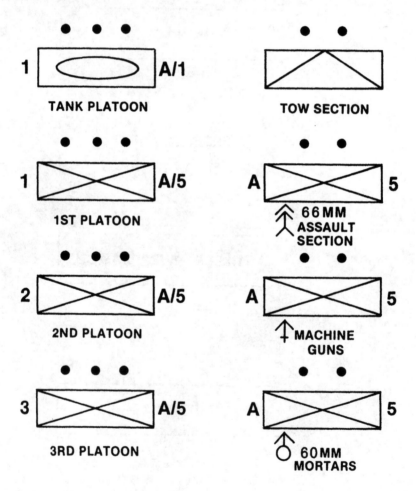

TANK PLATOON

TOW SECTION

1ST PLATOON

66 MM ASSAULT SECTION

2ND PLATOON

MACHINE GUNS

3RD PLATOON

60 MM MORTARS

Solution to Exercise Number 3

An inspection of the map will show a very simple depiction of
the concept of surfaces and gaps. It is purposely over-simplified
to keep the concept at the fore. Notice Hill 347. It is a strong
point. A well-defined, dug-in enemy is there. Therefore, it is a
surface. Beneath is a 120 millimeter mortar position. To you, an
infantryman, that represents a gap. Undefended by infantry, it is
vulnerable to your capability. Therefore, if you get in close
around it, you have an enemy weak spot. Next down, you have an
enemy tank position. Clearly, this is a surface. But right next
to it is an undefended command post, a tent camp; a gap. And then
you have a dug-in enemy position on a hill, again, a surface. So
from north to south you have surface, gap, surface, gap, surface.
Your first requirement was to use an arrow to indicate your main
effort. One good solution would be to point it at the 120
millimeter mortar position. This is a gap and you always want to
direct your main effort at enemy weakness.
There is an alternative solution. That would be to put your
main effort against the enemy command post, again a point of
weakness. If you did that you should not have difficulty
supporting your solution with rationale.
However, if you directed your main effort against either enemy
strong point or against the tanks you have not caught onto the
idea of directing your main effort against the enemy's weakness
intead of his strength. You put strength against strength.
So there are two alternate solutions. The 120 millimeter
mortars and the command post. The 120 millimeter mortars may be
the better solution for this reason. You can direct your main
effort in an attack against them and probably get away with it.
There is a treeline between that position and the enemy strong
point on the hill. However, if you attack the enemy command post,
though you are attacking a gap, notice how easily the tanks can
come and deal with you. Notice how much difficulty they would
have in getting up to the mortar position.
Once you destroy the mortar position, you will probably shift
your main effort and you will probably shift it to be against the
command post. You will also probably shift it after the enemy
tanks back off and begin to counterattack at the mortar position.
That way you can keep the enemy reacting to you.
The next requirement was to show a pinning force of some sort.
A good approach is to direct it against the enemy tanks because
you want to pin them down to deny them the mobility to come over
and deal with you. They represent the enemy's mobility. Even if
you put your main effort against the enemy command post, you
should still look for a pinning force to keep the tanks in place.
The next requirement was to show the location of your
reserves. One place for them consistent with the above actions is
on the hill mass of Hill 282. It may look strange to you that the
reserves actually are forward of the main effort and the pinning
force. But if they are so placed, they are in a position so that
if the tanks do go around behind 282, pass to the west of 282, and
come in where the enemy mortars are being destroyed, they then

expose their flank to the reserve. You could take advantage of that opportunity and attack them from the high ground with anti-tank weapons. You want the reserve to be in a position where it can take advantage of opportunities as they arise. In the event the tanks do pass around to the mortars, you may be able to use the reserve to attack the enemy command post. Remember, the reserve is there not to reinforce failure but to take advantage of opportunity.

The next requirement was to show one arrow depicting a target against which you would employ your artillery. A good solution is to employ the artillery against the northern enemy strong point. The reason is that you want to suppress that strong point while you direct your main effort against the mortars. It is important to realize that everything here is supporting the main effort. That includes the artillery. It does not mean the artillery has to be firing on the mortars. By firing on the infantry over-looking the mortars the artillery suppress that infantry so that it cannot interfere with the main effort that is directed against the enemy mortars.

You also had the opportunity to draw one arrow directed at a target that you would attack with your aviation. You might want to direct it against the enemy tanks. The tanks are vulnerable to aircraft and, again, you support your main effort by keeping the tanks engaged and apart from the forces of your main effort.

The next requirement is to show what forces you designated your main effort, what forces you put in your pinning force, and what forces you put in your reserve. One interesting approach is to make the tank platoon, and only the tank platoon, the main effort. With a platoon of tanks you can easily destroy a mortar position. You cannot hold that position with tanks alone. Holding the position is not the purpose, however. The purpose is destroying the enemy. You may have wanted to put infantry or infantry and tanks. But mounted infantry is extremely vulnerable with it is inside vehicles. LAVs are aluminum. They can be destroyed by heavy machine guns, and because they are aluminum, if they are hit with a heat round, they ignite on the inside and the troops burn. So you certainly do not want mounted infantry there with your tanks. Nor do you want your infantry to dismount and run around in the mortar position, because if they do that they sacrifice speed. It is going to take quite a while to gather them up and get them together again and move out. Anyone who has ever served in the infantry need only close his eyes for a moment and conjure up a vision from real-]ife of troops all over everywhere, trying in vain to get organized. You do not want that. You want a lightning blow to take out the mortars and be ready to shift the main effort elsewhere. So the tank platoon is the best main effort.

Now, the pinning force. You would probably do well to take a platoon and put it in the woods, as shown on the diagram, up close to the tanks. Not back on Hill 165, but in the woods so that the tanks cannot come forward. Those woods are going to be infiltrated with your infantry carrying anti-tank weapons. You could put your TOWs and Dragons in there as well so that the tanks simply cannot move forward of their position. You should bring along anti-tank mines as well. The Russians certainly would! Now the tanks only have one way to go and that is backward and that is where they are going to be hit by the air. The two remaining rifle platoons could be the reserve. The vehicles should be with them as close as possible. This way you have a mobile reserve and a large reserve, a reserve that can give the Sunday punch, that will provide the decisive quick victory that you want to achieve.

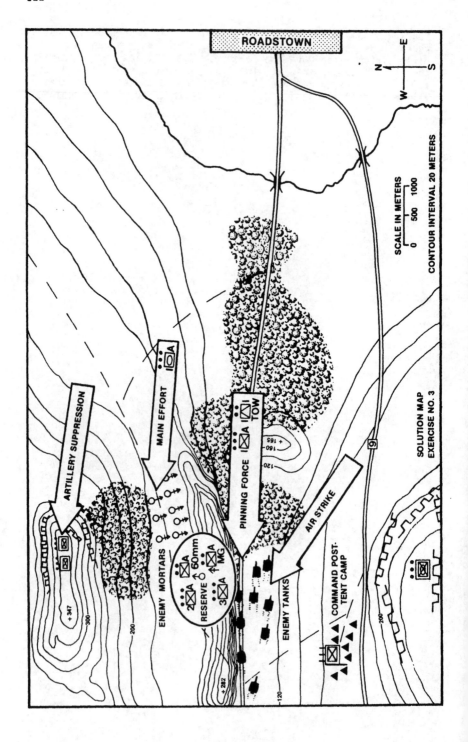

ROADSTOWN

SCALE IN METERS
0   500   1000

CONTOUR INTERVAL 20 METERS

ARTILLERY SUPPRESSION

MAIN EFFORT

PINNING FORCE

AIR STRIKE

ENEMY MORTARS

RESERVE

ENEMY TANKS

COMMAND POST-
TENT CAMP

SOLUTION MAP
EXERCISE NO. 3

Lecture IV:
The Concept of the Objective

According to the Joint Chiefs of Staff Publication Number 1, Dictionary of Military and Associated Terms, the objective is "The physical object of the action taken, e.g., a definite tactical feature, seizure and/or holding of which is essential to the commander's plan." That definition is clear enough.

Basil Liddell Hart would have disagreed with the JCS definition. At one point in his writings, Liddell Hart stated, "The only real objective is the enemy." Liddell Hart's statement is also quite clear and understandable, especially when we realize that whether we are attacking or defending, the problem is always the enemy. Once the enemy is taken out of action, defending and attacking are no longer necessary.

But the word objective has created a tremendous amount of confusion because the JCS dictionary definition is not the only one we use. Some officers deny that they have ever been confused by the term objective. Yet, if one discusses it with them, invariably it becomes clear that they are unsure what is meant and that the word takes on different meanings in different contexts.

Essentially, there are three different ways in which the term is used in the American military. First, it is defined in conformance with JCS Publication Number 1 as the physical end towards which we direct our efforts. However, if one refers to FMFM 6-4, the Marine Corps Doctrine for the Marine rifle company and platoon, he will find that "objective" appears in a list of tactical control measures, along with zone of action, boundary, line of departure, attack position, axis of advance, direction of attack and phase line, So now, according to FMFM 6-4, we are using the term objective to denote a control measure. FMFM 6-4 defines the control measure, objective, this way: "An objective is a locality or geographical feature to be captured or reached in the course of an attack. Assigned objectives must be seized and controlled."

The definition goes on from there and we will come back to it and deal with it. But, first, look at this lead sentence of the definition. It is necessarily a locality or geographical feature. This denotes terrain. It cannot be reconciled with Liddell Hart's view that the enemy is the objective. And then, in the next sentence, we learn that any assigned objective--the terrain so designated--must be seized or controlled. If we go back to our discussion of mission tactics, and consider the ever-changing enemy situation on the battlefield, we discover that anytime we define objective as does FMFM 6-4, we automatically build rigidity into our operations. We now have a locality or geographical feature which must be seized or controlled!

Many Marines will argue that our doctrine does not insist upon the objective being terrain. Yet, on reading FMFM 6-4, one is convinced otherwise. The definition continues: "Objectives may be: (a) Terrain which dominates all or the major portion of the company or platoon zone of action or axis of advance and, which, if occupied by the enemy, would jeopardize the accomplishment of the mission. (b) Terrain from which a subsequent coordinated attack will be launched. (c) Terrain required for purposes of controlling the attack as in areas where observation is limited or where distances involved require displacements of supporting weapons." Notice that in each of the three options provided, the first word is "terrain!" Terrain, therefore is clearly, according to Marine Corps Doctrine, the sole objective. And going back to FMFM 6-4's dictum that assigned objectives "must be seized and controlled" we seem to be being guided towards a set-piece battle in which we are to seize and control terrain rather than go out and defeat the enemy.

But there is yet a third use of the term objective that is in our military and doctrinal vocabulary. Objective is one of our principles of war. FMFM 6-4, contains a list of principles of war. The principle of the objective is defined as follows:

"The objective of a military force is the goal or aim usually expressed as a mission for which the force was constituted. This principle is overriding. It is applicable to any operation at any level of command. The objective of a force can be stated in either broad or precise terms depending upon the nature of the goal. Each element of an infantry unit contributes to the attainment of the objective of the larger unit of which it is a part. For example, when the objective of a battalion has been defined, all elements of the battalion must be assigned objectives that facilitate the attainment of the battalion objective. Success in combat is measured by the accomplishment of the mission.

So now the FMFM 6-4 has led us to further confusion by merging the definition of objective with that of the mission. The irony of the whole issue is that the principle of war, objective, is supposed to be the one that gives us focus and makes our purpose clear. However, the very word does quite the opposite. Its definition remains hazy. Therefore, it needs some clarification.

In a conversation that I had with a former Wehrmacht colonel, he cleared the issue up for me considerably this way:

In German we have the same control measure objective. If I speak to you in English, I call it the "objective." Speaking in German, however, I would not refer to the terrain as the Objektiv. That would imply that the terrain would be the whole object of effort. In German, the terrain that you designate as objective would be called the Angriffsziel, or the aiming point for the attack. The Angriffsziel, or aiming point, might change in the course of battle, especially, if the enemy is mobile. It is the enemy, then, that is the Objekt of our efforts.

The terrain, of course, is extremely important. We must use it to gain advantage. But the object of the attack is the enemy. The objective must be to take the enemy out of action, to destroy him, to disarm him. We cannot do that simply by seizing a piece of terrain and holding it. We must be prepared to move continually, wherever necessary, to confuse and disrupt him through a combination of fire and movement.

Since the word objective is so common it is not practical in this little lecture to attempt to eradicate it. We use it as a control measure. We use it in a way a German uses the Angriffsziel. Therefore, in this work, when the term objective appears, it means the aiming point, that towards which we direct our efforts in order to best use the terrain to accomplish our final goal: the destruction of the enemy. If, however, you prefer the term "aiming point" that is certainly acceptable.

It is best not to restrict the term objective solely to terrain, however. Therefore, in order to give the definition a little more breadth, let it be defined as:

The physical end towards which our efforts are directed.

"Mission" should not be confused with "objective." In this book we have dealt with mission under mission tactics. Objective will be an aiming point. Objective as stated under mission tactics will often be selected by subordinate commanders on their own within the scope of the mission assignment. The mission is to prevent the enemy from crossing the river. A suitable objective might be a bridge or a ford or a hill overlooking the river. It might be a hill overlooking the enemy. Which of these objectives is the most suitable may be a thing only the subordinate can determine after he arrives on the spot. He must have direction on his way to the river in question. When he moves out from his position, his objective may well be the bridge. But before he arrives there, he may find it appropriate to change his objective to the river or the ford. The objective may change in the course of battle. One should not be reluctant to change this control measure.

The ability to wisely select an objective is the mark of a good commander. The inability is the mark of an amateur and history is replete with examples of poorly selected objectives. There were hills fought for bravely by Marines in Vietnam after they ceased being of any tactical value. Lives were thrown away for meaningless terrain, terrain that did not meet either of the main criteria for selecting an objective. The two main criteria are (1) that it be useful to you; or (2) dear to your enemy. If it is neither one of these it probably is not worth the life of a single Marine. A good commander will, therefore, select terrain

that is useful to him. The great commander will have the ability
to select terrain that is dear to the enemy.

It may be useful to look at it from a strategic standpoint,
because the examples at that level are more written about and are
often more easily grasped by the student who has previously
studied history but not tactics. Consider our strategic examples
in Vietnam. All of our objectives were in the South. The South
was not dear to our enemy, the North Vietnamese. What we did in
the South was not of great concern to him. Therefore, he was able
to continue to plan calmly and reasonably his campaign against us.
When Douglas MacArthur landed at Inchon in 1950, he had selected
an objective that was dear to the enemy. MacArthur's objective
was Seoul. Seoul was behind the North Koreans' lines and it
controlled their lines of communication. Therefore, when the
North Korean army suddenly discovered that they had lost the
communication routes through Seoul, they became completely
disrupted. General MacArthur had taken something that was dear to
them. In so doing, he defeated them.

Now let us bring this discussion down to the tactical level.
Notice the diagram.

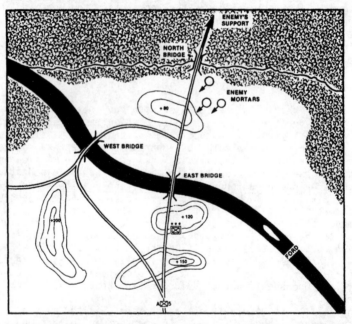

You, the company commander, Company A, 1st Battalion, 5th Marines,
are confronted by an enemy infantry platoon presently on Hill 120.
There are several potential objectives for you to select. There
is Hill 150 to his South. There is Hill 200 to his West. There
is the west bridge and the east bridge. There is the road
junction north of the east bridge. There is Hill 80. There is a
mortar position and there is a stream to the north end of the map.
What do you select as your objective?

There are several correct answers. Many might want to select the east bridge because that would tend to isolate the platoon from its support base. But those who are a little bolder might go all the way in to Hill 80, because that dominates the mortar position and, thereby, you could take away something very dear to the enemy, namely his mortar support. However, you might select the mortar position itself if you think you can move a force through the stream bed and surprise him from the rear. This would be a judgment you would have to make on the ground. If you selected Hill 150, however, you have taken something that might be a little bit useful in exchanging fire with the enemy, but something which is not dear to him. If you selected Hill 120, it looks as if you are going to merely engage in a battle of attrition. If you selected Hill 200, you have taken something that is of little value to either force.

Notice that probably the best objective was not a piece of terrain. It was the enemy mortar position. Objectives, even though they serve only as aiming points, should not be limited to pieces of terrain. Sometimes terrain is of essential value and it certainly should not be discounted. But consider other times, especially when both forces are mobile. Then it may be appropriate that the objective be an enemy force, enemy equipment, an enemy installation or the like.

If both forces are very mobile, terrain objectives can still be of the utmost importance. The tank commander, seeking to destroy an enemy column of trucks, may well want to select as his objective a piece of terrain that dominates a road over which the trucks will pass at a future time. The tank commander's mission will be to reach that objective at a time ahead of the column of enemy trucks. Or he may want to place his tanks at a position slightly short of that objective and move up onto the objective at the decisive moment in order to surprise the enemy trucks.

Selection of objectives, then, becomes one of the greatest challenges for the mind. The commander is trying to determine what thing, if captured, will be most disruptive to his particular enemy. Because not only do we want to defeat the enemy, we want to defeat him as rapidly as possible, and at a cost of minimum casualties to ourselves.

The commander must use caution, however, in assigning objectives to his subordinates, especially terrain objectives, lest they restrict the subordinate's latitude. It is an easy trap to fall into to think that you know the answers and send your subordinate units off in various directions, after which they will find themselves arriving at locations that are no longer relevant to the achievement of your goal.

Therefore, assign missions, not objectives. Sometimes objectives are very helpful in giving direction. One technique, however, is to use the term "reference" as opposed to "seize and hold." In other words, "Attack the enemy mortar position, reference Hill 80," rather than, "Seize Hill 80 and attack the enemy mortar position." This term, "reference," tells the subordinate that he should generally guide on this terrain you have selected, but it places him under no obligation to actually seize it. He can make that determination when he arrives on the spot. Any time you find yourself using the phrase "seize and hold" think twice. You are fixing your operations on terrain. Sometimes it is appropriate to do so. But often it is not and it deprives our operations of the fluidity that they may require in order to outfight the enemy. "Seize and hold" appears in thousands of example operation orders used over the past decades in Marine Corps schools and exercises.

Lecture V:
The Concept of the Reserve

General J. F. C. Fuller of the British Army, the original
author of the nine principles of war that the U. S. Army was to
adopt in the 1920's, once stated that of all the principles he
developed, the most important was economy of force. He reasoned
that whichever side still had forces left after the other side's
had been committed was bound to win. Napoleon seems to have had
similar thoughts when he observed that whoever still had his
<u>reserve</u> remaining after his enemy had committed his reserve, would
win the battle.

Presuming there is some truth to what Generals Fuller and
Bonaparte said, a commander should retain a fairly large portion
of his forces in reserve. As we observed before, the art of war
has no traffic with rules. A useful guideline, however, is to
keep approximately two thirds of your force in reserve whenever
possible. This would dictate, then, a change of thinking from
"two up and one back" to "one up and two back."

To commit a large number of forces early in the battle may
gain some early advantages. You may thereby surprise and shock
the enemy. You may inflict a large number of casualties. And you
may drive him off some important terrain. But if you have no more
reserves after you do this, you will not be able to sustain your
successes. Especially this will be true if the enemy has been
wise in retaining a large reserve himself.

The advantage of maintaining a large reserve goes further. As
you are always trying to deduce what the enemy is going to do, he,
likewise, is trying to figure out the same thing about you. If
you commit few of your forces, you telegraph less to him about
your intentions. You may not have fully made up your mind about
how you will commit these reserves. In fact, you should have a
multitude of different ideas about how to use them, based on the
multitude of different things the enemy may do. This may be what
Napoleon meant when he said:

> If I appear to be always ready to reply to everything, it is
> because, before undertaking anything, I have meditated for a
> long time--I have foreseen what might happen. It is not a
> spirit which suddenly reveals to me what I have to say or do
> in a circumstance unexpected by others--it is reflection,
> meditation.

What Napoleon was saying was that thorough thought in advance prepared him to make split-second decisions when the situation suddenly changed. Certainly thought in advance about the many situations that might occur would help in making the right decision fast about whether or how to commit the reserve. You cannot know which situations will occur. Nor can you know when the situation will change. So, you hold back a reserve. If you have made few or no commitments, you have given the enemy little or no information about your intentions.

This is not to suggest that you wait and cede initiative to the enemy. It does suggest that you use no more force than necessary to accomplish your initial goals. It also puts you in the position of being ready for the unexpected, an essential thing to be ready for, realizing that the unexpected is the common experience of war. A commander who cannot deal with the unexpected will probably not last very long.

Often examples of operation orders that appear in manuals as well as actual operation orders that have been used will have as the most prevalent mission assigned to their reserve, "be prepared to assume the mission of" some other unit. Such a mission given to a reserve shows no imaginative thinking whatever. To begin with, to assume the mission of attacking units is always an implied mission for any reserve anyway. So why even bother to list it? It is not often the best way to use the reserve. It almost connotes that one of your attacking units is going to fail, and that if it does, you are going to send in another unit, your reserve, where that unit failed. To do so has often been called "reinforcing failure." Reserves should not be used to reinforce failure. If one unit is in a position where it has become so vulnerable that it is sustaining heavy casualties, the chances are another unit thrust into the same position will meet the same difficulties. Even if you build up your "strength" by putting more and more men in the same area, you may not be increasing your combat power at all. You may just be giving the enemy a larger and larger target.

A careful study of the battle for Tarawa in November of 1943 shows a gross misuse of reserves. Three different battalions were committed singly, one at a time, along the same approach to the same beach. Each met with the same disastrous results. By the time that the last battalion was committed on that beach, the Japanese had lots of practice. Study of the operation order that was issued showed that the only missions assigned the reserve battalions were to assume missions of other battalions, in other words, assuming that the first battalions committed were going to fail.

A mission such as "be prepared to attack and cut the road at point A in the event the enemy begins to withdraw in that direction" followed by "be prepared to helo lift to Hill 232 in order to destroy enemy reinforcements if they appear on the Ridge Road," would show imaginative thinking on the part of the commander. It also shows that he is planning for several eventualities. He is preparing himself to deal with the unexpected. He has prepared his reserve commander to begin thinking of some of the possible uses that he may be committed to.

In other words, the reserve is going to be used to ensure success, not reinforce failure.

This is not to say that the reserve cannot be used to accomplish some mission you did not foresee. Use your reserve to seize on opportunities. Use the reserve in case of success, to exploit success, even if the appearance of success has surprised you. Commitment of your reserve is your bid for victory.

It is usually best not to commit the reserve piecemeal. The reserve is the Sunday punch, the violent stroke unleashed at the decisive moment. The ability to know, sometimes to sense, when that decisive moment has occurred, and where the decisive point is, is the mark of genius. The commander should always be watching for and anticipating this decisive moment. When it comes, it is time to commit perhaps all the forces available. To make the commitment too soon or too late can result in failure to accomplish the mission.

Once again, it is best not to establish a rule. Some say never to commit a part of the reserve without committing the whole thing. Such a rigid rule would, under some circumstances, fly in the face of economy of force. One commits what is needed, nothing more. However, one wants the reserve to be saved for a decisive stroke and all that strength is kept back there so that when the decisive moment comes, we will win quickly, once and for all and be able to move on to the next battle or phase of the operation.

Especially here in the age of helicopter transportability, however, there can be some very good reasons for committing a part and not all of the reserve. When helicopters are available, and when in command of a force, part of which is helicopter transportable and part of which is not, a commander should at all times be thinking about the eventuality of an opportunity for the heliborne commitment of his reserve. Therefore, under these circumstances, it is the wise commander who will constantly have in mind which portions of his reserve can go by helicopter and which cannot. The situation may well dictate that the helicopter transportable portion be separated out and committed by itself. But a more powerful commitment may be obtained in some circumstances by foregoing the use of the helicopter in order to take advantage of the increased combat power that might be available through the use of tanks and self-propelled artillery.

Once a reserve has been committed, the commander immediately sets about reconstituting his reserve. There is a right way as well as a wrong way to do this. Let us think on the level of the battalion commander for the moment. He is attacking with Company A. He has Companies B and C in reserve. The enemy exposes his flank and the battalion commander sends B and C together against the enemy flank. He now must reconstitute his reserve. The wrong way would be to start thinking about using supply personnel, weapons company personnel, communicators, etc. What he should be doing is watching closely to determine which of his three companies is the least committed. The reserve should be the least committed units. There may be times when no unit is completely uncommitted. Yet, the commander wants to have a reserve always available in order to exploit every opportunity as soon as it arises. In the situation described, it may be that although

Company A was used initially to engage the enemy, now Companies B
and C have been sent in for the decisive blow against the flank;
so, of the three, Company A is now least committed. The
commander's task, now, is not to begin forming a reserve unit out
of his communications and supply personnel, whom he needs to
sustain the battle. To do that is too much like a last ditch
effort. His task is to extricate Company A which may no longer
have a decisive function. The first task is to designate Company
A as the reserve. The second is to get it out of combat as soon
as possible. Once he does this, because he strives to keep
approximately two thirds of his force in reserve, his next task
may be to extricate either Company B or C. As soon as the enemy
appears to be routed, he can do this. He now has a reserve again
for the stated purpose of being ready to exploit opportunities as
soon as they arise. A reserve is not kept out of action waiting
to forestall some disaster. That absolutely is not its purpose.

To this point we have discussed how the commander can employ
his reserve. Let us now put on the shoes of the reserve
commander. He may be the senior commander of several units that
are kept in reserve, he may be the executive officer. Whoever he
is, his main task before being committed is to remain abreast of
the situation. A useful technique to insure this is for the
reserve commander to move with and be present with his commanding
officer through the course of battle. He may leave the reserve
forces under his executive officer or second-in-command so that he
is constantly with the overall commander or in the overall
commander's command post, keeping abreast of the situation. Then,
when the reserve is committed, his second-in-command may be
instructed to begin moving the reserve to a designated point where
the reserve commander will meet them.

It is necessary to make clear at this point something about
the special status of the reserve commander compared to commanders
of attacking units. It has to do with mission orders and the high
degree of initiative that we expect of subordinates. Say that you
are the regimental commander. Your reserve commander belongs to
you. Your attacking battalions are proceeding at their own
initiative, exploiting every opportunity. They are committed.
They are going. But the reserve belongs to you. It is your
responsibility to choose the decisive moment. In that way, you
have the opportunity to exercise your genius and win, or to show
that you are not a genius that day and lose. And you take
responsibility for it.

Let us not establish a rule here. There can be circumstances
where you may want to assign your reserve to an area and assign it
a mission to attack if such and such occurs. But this is not the
norm. You are responsible to be the genius, when it comes to
committing your reserve at the decisive moment.

In field exercises that have been conducted in Marine
battalions over the last several decades, it is generally the
least aggressive, the least experienced or least competent
commander who is assigned the mission of the reserve. It is time
that this thinking changed. The reserve is being saved for the
decisive moment and very likely it should be the most competent of
the commanders because it is the reserve commander who is going to

be called upon to win the battle. Any psychological stigma that is attached to being held in reserve should be eradicated. If it exists, it is a clear symptom that the unit in question and its commander are unaware of the true function of reserve. A study of history of great commanders, Frederick, Napoleon, Julius Caesar, Gustavus Adolphus, will show the ability to know the decisive moment and the patience and discipline to keep one's forces out of action until they are required.